TAPPY

From Barry Town to Arsenal, Cardiff City and Beyond

W0007686

Terry Grandin was born in 1941. He is married to Rita, has two children, Sarah and Jason, and four granddaughters Ella, Freya, Lauren and Tillie, with another grandchild due around the time of publication.

He was educated at Cardiff High School and completed his studies at the University of Wales Institute of Science and Technology, Cardiff.

He played in Newport County's youth team in the late 1950s and continued to play local football – for Cardiff Hibernian – until reaching the age of fifty.

A sports journalist, statistician and member of the Welsh Football Writers Association, his first book entitled Red Dragons in Europe was published in 1998.

TAPPY

From Barry Town to Arsenal, Cardiff City and Beyond

Derek Tapscott with Terry Grandin

Vertical Editions

Copyright © Derek Tapscott and Terry Grandin 2004

The right of Derek Tapscott and Terry Grandin to be
identified as the authors of this work has been asserted in
accordance with the Copyright, Designs and Patents Act,
1988

All rights reserved. The reproduction and utilisation of this
book in any form or by any electrical, mechanical or other
means, now known or hereafter invented, including
xerography, photocopying and recording, and in any
information storage and retrieval system, is forbidden
without the written permission of the publisher

First published in the United Kingdom in 2004 by
Vertical Editions, 7 Bell Busk, Skipton,
North Yorkshire BD23 4DT

ISBN 1-904091-09-1

Jacket design and typeset by HBA, York

Printed and bound by the Cromwell Press, Trowbridge

CONTENTS

Throughout my playing career and since my retirement, I have had the love and support of Glen my wife, and Karen and Jayne, our daughters. But I would like to dedicate this book to my three grandsons Gareth, Jamie and Haydn and hope that they enjoy reading about my life as a footballer in the 50s and 60s as much as I have enjoyed telling the tale.

Derek Tapscott

ACKNOWLEDGEMENTS

This book would not have been possible without the writing skills of my good friend Terry Grandin. Glen and I would like to thank him for his patience over the six months or so we have worked together on this project.

The majority of the photographs have come from my own collection but many thanks to Richard Shepherd for providing some from my days with Cardiff City.

Derek Tapscott

1

THE DAY MY LIFE CHANGED

It was bright and clear on the last day in September, 1953 when a well-dressed man stepped off the bus in Broad Street, Barry and walked around the corner into Queen Street. When he reached number 48 he stopped, marched up to the front door, and banged on the knocker. From that moment my life changed forever because the man outside my house was Barry Town's manager Bill Jones.

My mam heard the knock while she was in the kitchen. With 16 children to look after she seemed to spend most of her time in the kitchen.

'Hello Bill,' she said. 'If you are after Derek he hasn't come home from work yet.' Mr Jones asked if he could wait as he had an important message for me.

'Come on inside and I will make you a cup of tea,' said mam.

Mr Jones went into the living room and sat down at the dining table drinking his tea while my mother carried on busying herself in the kitchen. He had probably only been waiting ten minutes when I arrived home as usual about 5.15 pm as it didn't take me long to walk from the council depot where I worked. I always came in through the front door, it was never locked in those days, and I was quite surprised to see him sat at the table when I went into the room.

I said hello and then asked if there was anything wrong.

'No, of course not,' he replied 'but I had to speak to you myself. I want you to meet me at Barry Station tomorrow morning in time to catch the 7.00 am train to Cardiff. From there we are going on the 8.00 am express to London.'

I couldn't quite grasp what he meant so I asked him if we had a Southern League game in the London area for the next night.

'No, all I will tell you at this time is that we are going for an interview. There is someone in London who wants to meet you. Make sure you are not late, bring some overnight things, and wear your best suit.'

Now that was a problem because I didn't own a suit, but I did have a decent pair of trousers and a jacket so I knew I would be smart enough for the trip. That night I couldn't sleep. All sorts of thoughts were going through my head. I had no idea why someone would want to meet me. After all I was only 21, had been in a variety of jobs, and only ever played senior football for Barry Town in the Southern League and the Welsh League. I spent most of the night going over everything that had happened in my life, searching for reasons, but I still couldn't understand why someone would want to interview me. I finally fell asleep thinking about my life as a young lad in Barry, how I got started in football, and how I had reached what turned out to be a turning point in my career.

I was born in our house in Queen Street on 30 June, 1932 and christened Derek Robert Tapscott. My mam Florence came originally from Gloucester and my dad Stanley's family were from north Devon. I had four older sisters, Vera, Pat, Violet and June.

My dad's parents lived close by in Princes Street. Dad was a coalman at first but he eventually left that employment to go and work in Turners Asbestos Cement factory in Rhoose, which was then a small village not very far away.

Our house was a three-bedroomed corner terrace house with two rooms and a kitchen downstairs. There was one bathroom and an outside toilet. If you think it must have been crowded with five children living there with their parents then what about with 16 children, because I eventually had ten sisters and five brothers to make us probably the biggest family in Barry, and maybe even in South Wales. But don't forget that although it was a big family by any stretch of the imagination, it was pre-war and families were generally larger in those days.

We developed our own sleeping routine. Mam and dad had two other beds in their room and three or four girls would be in one and the two youngest children would be in the other. The middle bedroom had four boys in one bed while the girls used the other bed. The back bedroom was for the girls as they grew older. Everyone knew their place and looking back on our time together I can honestly say that we didn't consider ourselves cramped up and hemmed in as we never knew it any different.

I began lessons at High Street Junior School in August 1936 when I was four. My sisters used to look after me and take me to and from school as it was only just up the road a few minutes from our house. I never took a great deal of interest in lessons during my early days in school but I do remember that they were happy times.

I was rarely ill as a youngster but I needed to have my tonsils removed when I was five and dad took me to Barry Hospital. He left me there saying he was going to Woolworths to buy me a train set, but he never came back to visit me. I was in hospital for two days but mam made sure she came in to see me whenever possible.

By now the family had grown. At the end of 1937 I had another five sisters, Sheila, Glenys, Barbara, Pamela and Dorothy and also a brother Alan so we now totalled 11 children. Pamela and Dorothy were twins.

All of us used to help dad load coal on to the back of the cart. One day the horse reared up and I fell off the back and split open my chin. I carry the scars of that accident even now.

While my dad was still a coalman he also had a contract in the summers to tow out the gangplanks to the pleasure boats waiting out on Barry Island for the day trippers. His horse and cart was just right for this job and all the family would be down on the beach helping out. They were great days.

Dad was always working, we hardly ever saw him. As well as the beach summer job he also had a Sunday papers distribution service. Instead of going to the shops for Sunday papers people would buy them from him and that meant he needed delivery boys and girls. So every Sunday for many years, and even after I had left school, we all delivered papers on a Sunday morning for him.

I was only seven when World War Two started. Barry Docks was a prime target for German bombers and Queen Street was very close to the Docks. Our gang would sneak through the docks to get out onto Barry Island and play ball on the beach. I always had a little ball wherever I was going. I used to play in and around the Docks during the war with my pals Johnny Prosser, Derek Coombs, Johnny Collins and my cousin Terry Bullock. Once we found a bomb crater and collected a whole load of shrapnel which we brought back to show everyone.

The beach itself had steel posts dug into the sand and we were told it was to stop enemy landing craft but that didn't mean much to us youngsters. We never appreciated the dangers because we rarely saw any soldiers.

We also found a way to sneak in to watch the cricket on Barry Island during the summers. Instead of paying at the front gate we made a little opening in the fence at the back and used to creep through to watch games after Sunday School.

On Sundays we all went to Windsor Road Congregational Church. It played a big part in my life as all my sisters were married there and it was the venue for my mam's burial service.

A big treat for us after church was when I was sent to my grandmother's to collect a big bowl of custard for us all to share. It was my job because I was the eldest boy, and that also meant I could scrape the bowl out after everyone had finished.

At the end of the war Queen Street had a huge street party with trestles all laid out in the road. By now the family had grown even more. I had another sister, called Brenda, and then three more brothers, David, Malcolm and Clive. So now we were 15 children. The youngest member of the family, Geoff, would be born in 1947 to make the Tapscott family complete. It was a happy time.

I was very lucky because I was the eldest boy in the family. That meant my clothes were all new, while my younger brothers had the clothes that I grew out of.

Christmas was a very special time for us. Although mam and dad had very little money, they made sure that we were never without presents. Mam used to wrap up little gifts for us, usually fruit or nuts or something like that, and give them to the neighbours to keep until Christmas Eve. Then she would collect them all after we had gone to bed and arrange them downstairs by the fire.

We always had a real Christmas tree which dad brought home a couple of weeks before the big day and we would all help decorate the tree.

We also used to make our own trimmings to hang up. We made chains and fancy loops usually from coloured crepe paper or even newspaper. One year I came down early and opened the curtains only to bring down some of the trimmings which caught fire on the open grate. I was in big trouble after that for a few days.

I suppose my first interest in playing football came after I had a paper round when I was about ten years old. My route took me around the hilly area of Queen Street, Princes Street, Porthkerry Road, Pontypridd Street and Lewis

Street. I always used to take a tennis ball with me and I would be kicking the ball from house to house as I delivered the papers. With so much practice I started to become quite good at controlling the ball and while it was nothing like playing with a real football at least it gave me confidence for later on. I also played football out in the street and was the main one responsible for breaking loads of windows. I smashed Mrs Brown's windows opposite us plenty of times but I had a cheeky grin and always seemed to get away with it.

It was about then that I began playing football for the school, but that came only after my mam was able to do a little bit of business with the mother of the school team's centre forward. He had outgrown his football boots while I had never even owned a pair. Mam paid two shillings (10p) for his old boots but because they were too big for me I had to roll up newspaper and stuff it in the toes before I could wear them. That was my first ever pair of football boots and I treasured them more than anything else I had ever owned. Even in those days I saw myself as a centre forward because I wanted to be involved all the time, and of course I liked scoring goals.

From the ages of 11 to 14, children moved to the senior section in High Street with boys on one side and girls on the other. I enjoyed school but was more interested in sport than science. Perhaps that's why I was picked every Friday to go to the Girls school and pump up all their netballs. I looked after the boys footballs as well.

There was a very embarrassing moment for me when I was thirteen and selected to play for the school team. My mam had to take my birth certificate to school so that my age could be verified. When she arrived at the school it was realised that my birth certificate stated quite clearly that I was a girl. For 13 years no one had noticed. She had to take me to the doctor who naturally confirmed that I was a boy and my certificate was altered by the registrar. All he did was cross out the word 'girl' and replace it with 'boy'. That certificate was to come back and haunt me later on.

In 1944-45 I had a trial for Barry Schoolboys but was never selected for the final eleven. In the meantime I kept on scoring goals for the school.

Once the war was over it was time to start thinking about leaving school and finding a job and so in 1946, at the age of 14, I left High Street School and began work as a delivery boy for a butcher in Holton Road, just past Thompson Street and opposite the public house. I had my own bike with a basket on the front and used to deliver the meat orders around the local area – well I did for a short period of time. When I began the job the butcher promised me time off on Saturdays for football but after a couple of weekends he stopped it so I left. Surprisingly enough mam agreed with me so I didn't get into any trouble at home.

I found another job straightaway working for Radio Rentals who were also in Holton Road directly opposite the butcher's shop. I was very happy earning £1 a week helping a repairman mend wireless sets as it gave me Saturdays off so I could play as much football as I wanted.

After a year of passing tools to my boss while he mended radios I suddenly decided that if I was going to make something of my life I needed better prospects, perhaps even an apprenticeship. I found a local builder who was looking for a 16-year-old lad and so began working on the building sites as an apprentice bricklayer. My football had also developed a little and I was now the regular top scorer for Barry West End Juniors who remained undefeated for two years.

Working on building sites in all weathers toughened me up no end but it was hard graft. The football was going quite well and I remember playing one game in the afternoon for West End Juniors and then a cup final for the first team in the evening, and we won both matches. Football was beginning to dominate my life as that particular week I played a match every night of the week as well as those two games on the Saturday.

I stuck at bricklaying for twelve months until I saw a job advertised by Barry Council. They needed a young man to become a sort of jack-of-all trades, and as working for the council would give me the job security and even better prospects that mam and dad wanted me to have, I decided to go for an interview and luckily enough was offered the job. It was 1949 and I was 17 years old.

2

FIRST STEP ON THE LADDER

I enjoyed working for the council. I went all over the Barry area with my boss carrying out repairs to council property and of course I still had the weekends and evenings for football. As well as improving my ball control I had also become very mobile and speed was to become a vital part of my game in the future. My scoring exploits for West End came to the notice of Barry Town and I was delighted when they asked me to sign amateur forms for the 1949-50 season, not long after I had started work with the council.

It was strange how their interest in me came about. I injured my knee playing for West End and it was suggested that I go up to Jenner Park to see Albert Gardiner, the Barry trainer, who would give me the right treatment. When I went to see him he said that they knew all about me and asked if I would like to sign for them. I was glad to accept because I had always supported my hometown club. I didn't receive any payment and in fact continued to play most Saturdays for Barry West End in the Barry League though I trained at Jenner Park a couple of evenings a week.

I had played for most of my short career at centre forward but as I only weighed about nine stone around this time, Barry decided that I was too small and frail for that position. They switched me to outside right and I am sure that decision helped me progress no end.

Ernie Carless was player-manager of Barry's Welsh League side. He was a marvellous coach, only small in stature but a great athlete. He was also an inside forward and very knowledgeable and he taught me loads about the game. He was also a more than useful cricketer and captained the Barry Cricket Club though previously he had played for Glamorgan. No matter who you were, Ernie treated you just the same whether young or old and being with him was a brilliant start for me.

In the Welsh League we played on all sorts of grounds all around the South Wales area. Some were in reasonable condition but a lot of them were poor surfaces that made good football difficult. This meant that you had to have other strings to your bow. There was no use trying to play good football on a rock-hard rutted surface so you had to develop other talents. It was a superb way to learn a footballer's trade. I was given plenty of bruises and batterings by big ugly defenders who liked nothing better than 'sorting out' young upstarts like me.

But that is how you learn to play the game. I am sure that the experience of playing halfway up mountains, or on sloping pitches where the sheep had to be rounded up before the match could start, stood me in good stead throughout my career. The ground at Aberdare was always muddy and uneven, I remember trips to Lewistown, Mardy, Trelewis and Treharris. We played one match at a place called, if I remember rightly, Gwynfi which was halfway up a mountain. The football pitch was the only flat area in the place. I had a couple of shots which went wide of the goals and it took about ten minutes for someone to run down the hill to retrieve the ball each time.

Before the end of the game Ernie had devised a plan to use if we went a goal up. I managed to score late on to put us ahead so for the final few minutes we just kicked the ball over the edge to waste time.

It was about this time that I decided to buy a new pair of boots so I went to Jack Petersen's sports shop in Holton Road and selected what I thought would be the right pair for me. They were nothing like you see nowadays. They had hard toecaps, leather support up over the ankles, and nail-on studs, and there wasn't much of a choice either.

I saw places I never knew existed during that first season in Division Two of the Welsh League, which was Barry's second team and I also made my debut in the Southern League side. They regularly had 4-5,000 spectators watching home games at that time including my mam and sisters, especially when I was playing. A girl from a few doors up in Queen Street also used to go regularly with her friend Glenys Laban. They would meet up at Jenner Park with a few other girls to watch the match. Sometimes Glenys could be seen selling teas in the little kiosk.

In October 1950, along with every other lad who reached 18 years of age, I received my call-up papers and early in December 1950 I left Barry to start the two years national service that everyone had to do at that time. I thought football would have to be forgotten for a while but how wrong could I have been.

I joined 'A' Squadron, 4 Training Regiment, Royal Engineers in Aldershot on the Thursday – saw the Commanding Officer on the Friday – and received permission to play for Barry Town against Headington (now Oxford) United on the Saturday, providing I was back in camp on the Sunday.

I found out later that the club had sent a telegram to the CO asking permission for me to play and I was delighted when he agreed to let me go.

I hitched a lift to Reading, caught a train to Headington where I met the Barry boys who I had only left two days earlier, and we went on to easily win the game 3-0.

It became even better as I travelled back to Barry on the team bus, stayed at home on the Saturday night, and returned to Aldershot on the Sunday. Some introduction to army life.

I became a member of the drill staff within three months of joining up. This meant I was in charge of all the new recruits while they did their 'square-bashing' which was the term used for marching up and down the parade ground. Eventually I was promoted to corporal.

Mam used to write regularly to me while I was away but I wasn't much of a letter writer, in any case I was home quite often.

I managed to get leave to play in a number of games for the club that season, sometimes with the Welsh League side and on a few occasions in the Southern League.

During my second season with the Welsh League lads we used to play in front of crowds of around 1,000 at Jenner Park. There was that many in the ground when I scored against Panteg in a 2-0 win not long after the start of the 1951-52 season. We went to the end of the year before losing our first match and led the table in December after beating former leaders Girlings, and we ended up winning promotion back to Division One.

Making a few appearances in the side around then was a young lad of 16. He was an inside or centre forward called Dai Ward. His father had played for Barry for many years. Dai went on to join Bristol Rovers and then Cardiff City and he also won a couple of full caps for Wales. Sadly he passed away a few years ago.

My football skills didn't go un-noticed in the army and I was selected to play for the regiment at outside right. We won the inter-squadron annual football competition in 1951.

Around Easter time 1952, a Tottenham Hotspur scout came to watch me in action for the regiment and after the game he invited me to have a trial with Spurs. Two weeks later I received a letter from the club with the match details and, luckily enough, the Army gave me the Wednesday off. The game was at Craven Cottage against Fulham in the London Midweek League. I hitched a lift to London and then caught a bus to White Hart Lane to join up with the other members of the side. While I was at the ground I met one of my all-time favourite players, the Spurs and Wales captain Ron Burgess. It was brilliant just sitting down and chatting about football with someone like Ron who had already reached the top of his profession.

I then travelled with the other lads on the Spurs bus to Fulham's ground on the banks of the Thames. I remember we won 2-1 in an uneventful game but I didn't get on the score sheet. Making his debut for Fulham in that match was a young inside forward called Johnny Haynes. Even at such a young age he was already spraying balls all over the pitch and you could tell that if he worked hard and kept himself fit he would go on to become a star player. I felt that I had played well enough in the match considering I had never met any of the Spurs players before but I never did hear anything more from White Hart Lane although they did say they would be in touch with me. I was disappointed at the time but it is all part and parcel of the football game. You cannot let experiences like that get you down.

Just before I left the army a young lad called Jim Fotheringham joined up. He was to turn up in very different circumstances later on in my career.

Unlike many lads who do their national service all over the country and even in other parts of the world, I went to Aldershot on my first day, and never left the place. The only disappointment I had with army life was not getting home for Christmas, but I could hardly complain about that as I had most weekends off during the season for football.

I thoroughly enjoyed my national service and it was a wrench to leave when my two years were up but regular football was waiting for me back in Barry. I also had an interest in athletics by this time because while in uniform I had been competing in mile, three mile and cross-country races. I was good at the longer distances and it helped me build up the stamina I was to need later on as a professional footballer.

I was demobbed in December 1952 and straightaway I became a regular member of the first team squad in the Southern League.

I signed my first contract for Barry Town on 10 February, 1953. It was for the sum of £3 per week with a bonus of £1.10s (£1.50p) for a Southern League win and 10 shillings (50p) for a win in the Welsh League.

Getting back into regular football for the club couldn't come soon enough for me because I knew that I would be playing with characters such as the great Stan Richards, Charlie Dyke, Bryn Allen, Ted Morris and the other mainstays of the Barry first team.

Stan Richards held the Cardiff City goalscoring record with 30 in a season until it was recently beaten by Robert Earnshaw. He also had a season with Swansea Town and scored a lot of goals for them but injuries were catching up with him. He was one of the best headers of the ball I have ever seen and I went on to play with, and against, many of the country's top centre forwards.

Stan would tell me where he was going to put the ball before he had even headed it. Of course by the early Fifties his legs had gone but he could still play. I did all his running for him but in the air he was out of this world.

As long as Stan had a couple of pints just before the match he would be fine. He never let the side down and no one worried if he did have a drink. He would quietly sneak off to the local pub, finish his beer, and then be back in time to change and go out on the pitch. I will never forget all the special training he and I did together. Ball after ball I would cross into the area where Stan would be waiting to spray those headers with pinpoint accuracy.

Charlie Dyke was another with a great personality. He had been a pro with Chelsea for three years and had only just dropped down to the Southern League. He taught me about wing play, ball control and taking corner kicks. Later on he would become manager at Barry and he gave tremendous service to the club.

It was Charlie and Stan who went in to see Mr Jones not long after I signed that first contract. They persuaded him to put my money up to £5 per week, win or lose, to bring me in line with the other members of the team.

Mam and my sisters continued to come and watch me playing for the Linnets, as Barry Town were known in those days. To me they will always wear green shirts and be the Linnets. I cannot get used to this new Dragons nickname, or their yellow jerseys. It just doesn't seem right. I suppose it must be the same for most older players and supporters.

The first match on my return from the army was against Exeter City Reserves in January 1953. Things looked black when we went a goal down but I was partnering Charlie who was on the right wing and we started to get back into the game. I helped Stan score a quick hat-trick and we went on to win 3-1. He was injured scoring his first goal but he stayed on the field, not moving around a great deal of course, and still managed to score the other two.

The following week I opened the scoring at Gravesend when I rounded their keeper but they hit us hard in the second half and went on to win 4-1.

It took me a while to get used to being back in civvy street. Of course the biggest change was at home where I returned to sharing a bed again after two years of sleeping on my own, but it was good to be back in Barry with all my family and friends once again.

The goals started coming regularly for me and at the end

of the 1952-53 season we beat Cardiff City 3-0 to win the South Wales Senior Cup. I scored two goals in that game and it was a big win for us because the City side contained about eight first team regulars. There was talk that the Bluebirds may be interested in signing me but the club was never approached by anyone from Cardiff City, even after we had beaten them in that cup final. I was told later on that the Cardiff management felt I was not good enough to make the grade at the higher level.

Training at Jenner Park consisted of endless laps of the pitch around the dog track followed by exercises. There was no gymnasium so everything took place outdoors, whatever the weather. I enjoyed the training. I think my time in the army made it much easier for me to keep myself fit.

Early in the 1953-54 season, on 26 September, we travelled to Stonehouse in the opening qualifying round of the FA Cup. It was not the first time that we had come up against the Gloucestershire side as we had played them a year or two previously so we knew what to expect from them.

Coachloads of fans left Jenner Park for Stonehouse and we had almost 1,000 supporters in the ground when play started.

It was end-to-end stuff at first but gradually we got on top and I cut in from the right wing to score the opening goal just before the half time whistle. I managed two more in the second half for my hat-trick but in scoring my third goal I collided with their keeper and had a nasty split just above my eye. Our trainer Albert Gardiner wiped it clean and put a plaster over the cut and I carried on playing. Bryn Allen, Charlie Dyke and Albert Stitfall also scored in the second half and so we went through to the next round with an easy 6-0 victory. On the journey home in the bus there was a lot of talk about which side we would have in the next round. I didn't know of course that in a few days time I would be on my way to London.

I was back at work for the council on the Monday and Tuesday and that night I went up to Jenner Park for some light training. We had been playing a few midweek games as well as the Saturday matches so training was low key. On the Wednesday I went to work as usual but came home to find Mr Jones waiting for me with his news of the London interview.

3

THE MARBLE HALLS

It took me about 15 minutes to walk to Barry Station and Mr Jones was waiting for me when I arrived. He had already purchased our tickets. I had with me an overnight bag which mam had packed containing a clean shirt and a few other items. She had also polished my shoes and was up early that Thursday morning to make sure I would be on time for the train.

Although I asked Mr Jones to tell me more, all he would say was that we were going to meet someone in London. 'You will find out soon enough when we get there,' he said.

When we arrived at Cardiff General we changed platforms and there, also waiting for the London train, was Mr John Bailey, the chairman of Barry Town. Then the train pulled in, we walked along the corridor until we found an empty compartment and the three of us sat down waiting for the journey to start.

When we reached the Severn Tunnel, Mr Jones said it was time to visit the buffet car.

Never before had I eaten bacon and eggs on the move, it was much better than the fry-up I had been used to in the Army. There were teas all round to wash breakfast down and it was very enjoyable, yet I still couldn't get any more information out of either Mr Jones or Mr Bailey who obviously also knew where we were going. All they talked about was their hopes and dreams for Barry Town such as ground improvements at Jenner Park, new dressing rooms, and better facilities for the supporters.

When we reached Paddington, Mr Bailey left for a

previously arranged business appointment and I followed Mr Jones who was heading for the Underground. As we reached the ticket office he said 'Two to Arsenal Stadium please,' and that was the first time I had any idea where he was taking me. I was flabbergasted that anyone at Arsenal would want to meet me. I could tell that Mr Jones had enjoyed keeping me in the dark as he had a little smile on his face. I asked him who we were going to meet at Arsenal and he said quietly 'Mr Tom Whittaker.'

I couldn't believe it. Arsenal were the biggest club in the country, the Football League champions, and he was one of the most respected managers.

We changed trains at Kings Cross and eventually got off at Woolwich Arsenal.

It was a big climb up to the street after arriving at our stop and on reaching daylight we had to ask someone the way to the stadium itself. We were told to go left, then first right, and halfway up the road we would find the main entrance.

When we got closer I could see seven stone steps leading up to glass doors and over the entrance was the Arsenal badge cut out in stone. Up higher was written the words 'ARSENAL STADIUM'. As we went up the steps the door opened and a gentleman in full uniform, his name I found out later was Len, asked us our business.

'We have an appointment with Mr Whittaker,' said Mr Jones quite proudly. We went in through the glass doors and into the main hall. Len telephoned the manager's office and Mr Whittaker's secretary, a very nice lady called Miss Grosvenor, came straight down to meet us. She welcomed us to Arsenal Football Club and then took us both upstairs to Mr Whittaker's office.

Miss Grosvenor took Mr Jones in first to introduce him to Mr Whittaker and then I was called in to meet the great man. He was standing behind his desk. His jacket was hanging up on a coat stand and he was wearing a black waistcoat. The office was panelled out in rich dark wood and there was a long window overlooking the main street to one side of his desk. There was a jug of water and some glasses on the desk which was covered in paperwork.

I must have looked a little the worse for wear because I still had the plaster over my eye following the knock against Stonehouse.

'How did you get that cut and how many stitches did you need,' was his first words to me. I told him that I never had time to get it checked at the hospital but Albert Gardiner, the Barry trainer, had fixed it for me. All Albert really did was wipe the cut clean with a sponge and stick the plaster over it.

'You look a little bigger than the reports I have received about you. We had you watched again at Stonehouse last Saturday and by all accounts you played very well.'

He was a big man, slightly balding and with heavy-rimmed spectacles but he put me at ease straight away and I soon felt at home. He wanted to know which position I preferred and I told him up front getting among the action and scoring goals, anywhere up there where all the hard work could be found. I have never been a dirty player but I was always very enthusiastic and liked 'getting stuck in'.

'We have followed you for some time and I have received good reports about you. Now, before we go and have some lunch there is something very important that I have to ask you. Would you like to join this football club?'

I couldn't believe it. I barely managed to stammer out that I would be delighted to join Arsenal as it must be every young player's dream to join such a great club.

With that the three of us went out of Mr Whittaker's office and down some stairs into the club restaurant where we sat at an empty table. We had a sausage and mash lunch which was brought to us, though normally everyone would go and get their own lunches. There were quite a few players sat eating at the same time but I was in such a daze that I cannot remember who was there.

When lunch was over, we went back to Mr Whittaker's office and I was sent out into the boardroom to wait while the two managers finalized details of the transfer fee. The boardroom was huge and there were cabinets full of trophies, caps and jerseys and I can still remember the boardroom table as it was so very highly polished. Every wall was panelled out in rich wood. Outside the boardroom there was a shield commemorating the hat-trick of championship wins between 1932 and 1935. It was all so different from anything I had ever seen before.

I was in the boardroom on my own for almost an hour until Miss Grosvenor brought me a cup of tea and told me that they wouldn't be much longer. I had just finished the tea when she came back to say they were ready for me in the office.

Mr Whittaker was sat at his desk when I went into the room and he said that he had agreed terms with Mr Jones. I found out later that Arsenal would pay Barry Town £2,000 for me and play a game at Jenner Park. If they were unable to meet that obligation the fee would increase to £3,000.

I was told that my wages would be £11 in winter and £9 in summer with added bonuses of £2 for a win and £1 for a draw. Top money in those days was £12 during the season and £10 in the summer so it was a good deal and I readily agreed, especially as I also received a £10 signing-on fee.

'The forms will be ready for you to sign at about 6.00 pm this evening,' he said.

The ground would still be open at that time as there was a charity match taking place at Highbury that evening between the Boxers and Jockeys. This was a regular event at the Arsenal and used to pull in huge crowds every year.

We didn't have to wait around for three hours or so at the club as they had booked a room at a nearby hotel for us. It was just up the street opposite the ground.

Mr Jones and I sat in the lounge of the hotel drinking cups of tea and chatting about football in general. He telephoned someone at Barry Town to let them know the situation and before long it was time to return to the club.

As we got to the main entrance the door opened and out came a footballer who I later found out was Bill Dickson. He had also signed forms that day and was a Northern Ireland international who had just left Chelsea to sign for the Gunners.

Mr Jones and I were escorted back to the manager's office where Mr Whittaker and Miss Grosvenor were waiting. The forms were on the desk ready for me so I signed straightaway. It was 1 October 1953.

Mr Whittaker stood up and came over to shake my hand.

'Derek, you are now an Arsenal player and you will be in the Combination side to play at Queens Park Rangers on Saturday.'

With that he sent for one of the trainers, Bert Owen, who took me down to meet a few of the Arsenal players who were still at the ground.

Jack Kelsey was first to come up and say hello. News must have got to him that I was Welsh. I found out later, when in digs with Jack, that he thought I was another goalkeeper as he had seen a photograph of me in one of the sports papers when I was wearing a polo-neck sweater.

Joe Mercer and Joe Wade also made me feel very welcome within a few hours of my becoming a Gunner.

We remained at the ground for the charity match and then went back to the hotel where we stayed the night before catching the 8.00 am train from Paddington back to Cardiff the next day. From Cardiff to Barry and then back home. When I reached our house mam and dad already knew what had happened as the local grapevine had been working overtime. It must have come from Mr Jones or his contacts at the club. Dad was as pleased as punch, as was mam, but she was a little upset at me finally leaving home because although I had been in the army for two years I had been able to get home almost every other weekend during my national service.

My only regret was that I was never able to say goodbye to most of my mates at Barry Town. Everything was in such a rush; it was quite hectic as I had to catch the train back to London early the next morning. I carried my boots in a carrier bag.

This time I was met by a member of the groundstaff at Paddington Station and he drove me to Shepherds Bush and the Rangers ground at Loftus Road. My career at the Arsenal was about to begin.

4

A FULLY-FLEDGED GUNNER

Jack Crayston came out to meet me when I arrived at the ground. He had met me when I first went to Highbury to see Mr Whittaker. He told me that when I went back to Arsenal he would ask Jack Kelsey to take me to my new digs. He also introduced me to the players and they all wished me the very best of luck. There was a shock in store for me when I met the Arsenal lads. Playing centre half was none other than Jim Fotheringham, the same Jim Fotheringham who had joined my regiment when we were both doing our national service. Big Jim was still in the Army and we had a laugh at meeting again under such different circumstances. Sadly Jim, who was a strapping centre half, passed away several years ago while still very young.

I was very surprised at the players attitude to the game – we are all here for just one thing – an Arsenal victory.

It seemed strange pulling on the famous red jersey with the white sleeves as we prepared to go out against QPR. My new team-mates soon made me feel at ease. Amongst them that day were Len Wills, Gerry Ward, Ray Swallow and wing Brian Walsh who I would join up with later in my career. Jim Standen was in goal for us.

We won 2-0 but I never opened my account although I did go close a couple of times.

It was much quicker than anything I had been used to before. If there had been substitutes in those days I would probably have been taken off, but I managed to last the game, even with the sticky plaster still over my eye from the Stonehouse cup tie.

After the match there was a bath or shower available for everyone. That was a bit different to Barry where we had to take it in turns to use the bath or the single shower. It seemed to me at the time to be the best shower I had ever had. Just before I left Loftus Road, Bert Owen, who looked after the kit, told me to see him when I got back to Highbury and he would show me the club's boot room.

At the end of the game I was taken to Paddington Station to catch the train back to South Wales. I was getting quite used to being a rail passenger. This time though Arsenal were paying the £2.10s (£2.50) train fare.

All my belongings were still at home and so I was given leave to travel back, collect my things, and then report to Highbury on Tuesday at 3.00 pm. All the way back on the train I couldn't get it out of my head that I was now an Arsenal player. I had a light snack while travelling, Arsenal would pay for that as well, and finally arrived in Barry in good time. On my way home to Queen Street, particularly on the stretch between the Barry Hotel and our house, everyone stopped me to ask about my move. It took me over an hour to get through the front door.

Mam had already washed and ironed a couple of shirts when I reached home later that night. She wanted to make me some supper but I told her that I had already eaten on the train. All my brothers and sisters were waiting to hear exactly how I had got on in London so that took a while as I remembered all that had happened to me including meeting some of my new team-mates.

So it was back to normal sleeping arrangements at home for a few days but I knew that the time had come to tell mam that from now on I would be staying in London and not coming home so often.

Over the weekend we collected everything she thought I would need but then on Monday we realised that I didn't have a case suitable to take to London. Once again my mother saved the day by nipping up the road to one of the neighbours who lent me a case on the understanding that the next time I came home I would bring it back.

On Sunday morning I walked up to Jenner Park because I knew that Albert Gardiner, Bill Jones and a lot of the players would be up there. I had to relate everything that had happened to me to the lads and it was three or four hours and a couple of cups of coffee before I left to walk back home.

Charlie Dyke knew Highbury as he had played there a number of times for Chelsea. He wished me all the luck in the world and I told him, and the others, that if it wasn't for them I wouldn't be at Arsenal. While I was there I was presented with a gold watch which all the Barry players and staff had chipped in for, Stan Richards made the presentation to me. It was a very emotional moment. He said he hoped that I would soon settle down at Highbury and play myself into the Arsenal first team. I thanked everyone for the kindness and encouragement given to me while I had been at the club.

I was at the ground so long that when I got in, mam told me off for being late. 'Just because you are a professional footballer with the best club in the land doesn't mean that I am no longer the boss,' she said as dad, as usual, sat quietly in the corner.

After dinner I went to see my granddad and for the third time since coming home recalled all that had happened to me.

On the Monday I went up to High Street School to say cheerio to Mr Jones and the other teachers and thank them for taking an interest in me during my early years.

Early Tuesday morning I said my goodbyes to the family, caught the train to Paddington, and then took the underground to Arsenal Station. I had breakfast before leaving home so there was no need to make use of the buffet car on this trip although I did go there to buy a cup of coffee. In my case, or rather my neighbour's case, were two shirts, a sweater, a jacket and some underclothes. I was wearing the only pair of shoes I possessed. Mam had also packed away shoe polish and brush, and soap and a towel.

There is only one way in to Highbury, and that is through the main entrance. One important rule for all players was that a jacket and tie had to be worn in and out of Highbury at all times, even if you were just there for training. It was all part of making the club something special.

I said good afternoon to Len who was on the door as usual and then quickly went up to see Miss Grosvenor as I had been told to bring my birth certificate so that the club could verify my personal records. After handing the envelope to her I went back downstairs and through a door on the right that was used by all the players. I walked down through a tiled corridor and past the away dressing room, which was also used by the reserves. The assistant secretary's small office was next, and then there was the physio's room before you arrived at the home dressing room. Both main dressing rooms had underfloor heating and the walls were tiled as well as the floor. The windows in the home dressing room looked out onto the main road.

I spotted Bert Owen in one of the rooms and he called Jack Kelsey out to see me. We had a brief chat and he said he would meet me after training to take me to our digs. Bert then gave me my first training kit which consisted of top, shorts, socks and training boots that were a bit like basketball boots. These would be put out every day for me, as they were for all the players, and they were all numbered so that you always received your own kit. He also gave me a chit to go to a specialist sports shop to choose a pair of football boots. I slowly changed into my new gear and hung my ordinary clothes on the hangers provided.

When I walked out onto the pitch to start training I had to stop for a moment and look around. The stands looked so huge, and who could fail to recognise the famous clock. It all looked so enclosed to me after being used to Jenner Park's surroundings.

I had one hour's training that day. I just did lapping around the pitch, twisting and turning every so often to keep my muscles supple. Bert stayed with me the whole time as I was on my own for this session.

When my work was completed I went back to the changing rooms where my own personal towels had already been laid out for me. A bath or shower was available and I chose a shower after stacking my training kit on the bench so that it could be collected, washed and ironed before being returned to me the following day. I then went looking for Jack as I was anxious to see what my digs were like.

He was having a cup of coffee with a member of the groundstaff who had been given the use of a club car to drive us to the digs. The lodgings were in Muswell Hill, about half an hour from the ground and situated at the top of a hill. At the bottom of the hill was Alexandra Park where they held horse racing meetings. The digs were above a clothes shop and the entrance was to the side of the shop. There were five or six bedrooms. I was to share one with Jack, Bill Healey, a former Arsenal and now Fulham pro was in another bedroom, and the others were taken up by the landlady Mrs Ring and her husband and daughter.

Bill didn't stay very long in the digs before being transferred from Fulham to Hartlepool, which was just as well because he was always riding a very noisy motor bike. He had originally been part of a swap deal that brought Bill Dodgin to Arsenal from Fulham.

The digs were on a bed and breakfast basis with evening meal and cost us £2.12s 6d (£2.62) each with the money deducted before we received our wages. If we went home on any weekend, the rent was reduced by ten shillings (50p).

Mrs Ring was a fabulous person. Nothing was too much trouble. She even did our washing and ironing and cleaned the rooms. The whole place was spotless.

In our room we had two beds, two wardrobes and a large chest of drawers. Luckily for us, we were situated in the front of the building overlooking the main road. Mind you, good as it was, it took me a long time to feel comfortable while I was there because I was used to three or four-in-a-bed and I had never before had so much space to myself.

Jack and I had a long chat after dinner on that first evening together. He told me all about the Arsenal and finished with some good advice. 'Don't do anything stupid and they will love you. Do your best for the club and they will do their best for you.' I slept well that night.

We went down for breakfast the following morning and Mrs Ring had prepared poached eggs on toast with lots of tea. There was no fried breakfast available as the club watched over your diet even in those days and Mrs Ring was obviously acting under orders.

We left the digs in plenty of time as we had to be at the ground by 9.30 am ready for training to start half an hour later. Jack and I caught the bus to Finsbury Park and walked the rest of the way.

By now I had already visited the sports shop with my chit from the club and selected a new pair of boots. In those days there were not the choices that are now available, in fact there were probably only a couple of different makes. I tried a pair of McGregor boots which I immediately liked so I decided to have those. Bert Owen would look after my boots along with all the others, putting a number on the soles to show who they belonged to. My number would be eight.

There was training every day of the week, 10.00 am until 12.30 pm, unless there were midweek games. First team and second team players all joined in together. There were various training areas. In the gymnasium you could do exercises or even a little weight training, though that was nothing like you have these days. At that time it was just bar bells to help improve upper body strength. Bill Watson was in charge of the gym.

Outside around the perimeter of the ground there was lapping the pitch and sprint work, and then behind the terracing and the big clock there was a five-a-side pitch where match tactics would be worked on. Alf Fields and Leslie Compton used to take the training with us.

If you needed a massage, or a good rub-down, Bert Owen and Billy Milne were the physios. Billy was like concrete, he was such a hard man. It was reckoned that he once played for Arsenal for the best part of a match with a broken leg.

All the more experienced players offered advice and help to us youngsters. The way they looked at it was that we were all Arsenal players and we all wanted the same thing – success for Arsenal Football Club. Tommy Lawton, Doug Lishman, Don Roper, Jimmy Logie and dear Joe Mercer all spent extra hours helping us younger lads improve our game. In fact Tommy had only been signed by the Gunners a fortnight or so before I joined the club yet his vast experience was to prove a big help to me.

He had a ball suspended at the end of the tunnel so that when we started training we all had to jump up and head it. He said that if we headed it properly, with our foreheads, then it wouldn't hurt. In those days the ball became very heavy in wet conditions and if you caught it in the wrong place, you were in for a headache. Tommy was always telling us what to do and what not to do. He and the other senior players would all try to put right anything that was wrong with our game. They all spent hours helping us though they didn't have to do it. That was the way they had learned the game. In Tommy's case it was from the likes of the great Dixie Dean at Everton.

I followed up the QPR match by playing the following week against Brighton at the Goldstone Ground but a shoulder injury in that game put me on the sidelines for five weeks. After the elation of joining the club and playing my first two games, having an injury so soon was a bitter blow.

I was sandwiched between their keeper and a big centre half and I felt the full force on my shoulder. I had to go off the field for a few minutes to get my breath back and Bert Owen gently eased my shoulder back in and strapped me up. I didn't think it was serious so after a couple of minutes I went back on and finished the game although perhaps in hindsight that wasn't the best course of action.

At the end of the match I somehow managed to shower and change but I couldn't even carry my bag to the bus in my right hand and a couple of the lads helped me to my seat.

The shoulder was very painful over the weekend and I had to go in to the club on the Sunday to see Billy Milne for treatment. In those days the heat lamp was used to reduce swelling and bruising and so every day, for what seemed like ages, I went in to see him and we had an hour's session. I didn't want to miss the next match but Billy refused to give me clearance. It didn't stop me training because as Billy said, 'It's only your arm, you have still got two legs.'

But it took a long time to recover and I was always wary of it even in later years.

It was a depressing time. I had nothing to do although it did give me the opportunity of watching the first team in action.

I was also now getting used to receiving my wages. Every Friday after training we would go to the main office where we each received a small brown pay packet with our names on containing our money. A new young lad called Ken Friar had just started in the office. We would remain friends even after I left the club. I had not realised it at the time but joining the great Arsenal from Barry Town cost me in my pocket. When you added up the money I received from Barry Council to that from Barry Town, I was £4 light when Arsenal paid me, and that was even before the digs money was taken out. Still, I didn't do too badly considering the top players at Arsenal like Doug Lishman and Tommy Lawton were only getting £1 more than me.

Once I regained my full fitness I became a regular member of the Combination, or reserve side and it was a great learning experience because it prepared me for the day I would start playing league football. The reserve side was pinned up on the notice board just as the first team line-up was and we held our team meetings in the dressing room before the matches.

All our home games were played at Highbury on Saturday afternoons and usually in front of crowds totalling between 10-15,000, depending on the opposition.

Con Sullivan, a goalkeeper from Bristol City joined us in February 1954 and he was also a regular member of the reserves. Con came to stay in the same digs with me when Jack Kelsey left to get married. Also in the side that first season were Brian Walsh, Danny Clapton and Jimmy Bloomfield.

I won the Arsenal crowd over by playing in every reserve match as if it was an international. Many times the older players and the training staff would tell me to temper my enthusiasm with a little caution but it was no use, that was the way I played the game.

I was lucky enough to be taken away with the first team for a few matches just to get experience. I went to the Manchester City, Sunderland and West Brom games and it was good to be involved amongst so many great players.

Back in the reserves the goals started going in and I was a regular scorer coming into the Easter programme. I had netted 13 goals in 15 appearances for the reserves but it was a place in the first team that I desperately wanted and little did I know that an opening was about to appear.

5

REACHING THE HEIGHTS

Unknown to me, when Mr Whittaker signed me he thought it would take about two years for me to learn my trade the Arsenal way. Circumstances meant that I was given my opportunity by the club just six months after leaving Barry Town.

In the first of a three-match home spell in April, 1954, Arsenal had been in a tough midweek encounter with Aston Villa, drawing 1-1 with a goal from Tommy Lawton. During the match, inside right Jimmy Logie was injured. As that game had been held on a Tuesday it didn't leave Jimmy a great deal of time to recover for the weekend. He was in with Bert Owen and Billy Milne all Wednesday and was still in the physio's room when we arrived for training on the Thursday.

I was just about to get into my training gear when I was told that Mr Whittaker wanted to see me. I immediately went down the corridor and up the stairs to his office and Miss Grosvenor asked me to wait while she told Mr Whittaker I was there. In next to no time he called me in to see him. He told me to sit down and then said that he had been very pleased with my progress in the six months since I joined the club.

'I am delighted to tell you that you are in the first team for the match against Liverpool here at Highbury on Saturday.'

I could hardly believe it. When Jimmy's injury failed to clear up I thought there might be a chance for me as he was inside right, the position I had been playing mostly in the reserves, but it was only a very slim chance. I was speechless but as always, Mr Whittaker understood my feelings.

'Just go out there and play your normal game,' he said. 'And by the way, your secret is safe with me and as long as you do your best for Arsenal Football Club then it will stay that way.'

I went bright red as I knew he was referring to my birth certificate that had been altered by the registrar. At last I was able to thank him and then I flew down the stairs and back to the dressing room as quickly as I could. When I got there the team had already been pinned up on the notice board and there at number eight was D Tapscott.

Every player came in turn to congratulate me and Joe Mercer sat by my side and calmed me down as he could see how excited I was at the prospect of making my First Division league debut.

'Just take things as they come and don't worry about making mistakes,' he said. 'Treat it as you would any other game you have played in.'

Training that Thursday was just a blur and in next to no time I was back in the digs with Jack telling me not to worry about anything. I still slept well that night.

It was a shame that I couldn't let mam and dad know that I was in the first team. They would eventually find out by reading the papers on the Saturday.

When Jack and I arrived for training the next day my gear had been laid out on the number eight peg. I put in a little extra during that morning session as I seemed to be bursting with energy and then, after showering and getting dressed, I joined the other players in the boardroom for the team talk by Mr Whittaker that was always held the day before any first-team game.

It was frightening sitting up there with players like Mercer and Lawton who were seasoned international stars. Everything about the opposition was discussed, their strengths and weaknesses and the style of play we would adopt to win the game. I was welcomed to the first team by Mr Whittaker and then told to listen to the players around me and do what I had been doing since I arrived at the club.

We all went to lunch and after that Jack and I caught the bus home. All Jack could say to me was don't worry as everyone on that field tomorrow had to make their debuts at some time or other. He said there were some great players in the Arsenal side and they would all look after me.

There was not even the remotest suggestion of nipping out for a celebratory pint of beer. After Tuesday nights no Arsenal player was allowed out, and that was strictly adhered to by everyone at the club from youngsters to senior professionals.

This time I did have a sleepless night. It was going to be far different for me playing in front of a 45,000 crowd than the 10-15,000 I had been used to in the London Combination League.

Jack and I were up early as usual and after a light breakfast, some toast and a cup of tea, we made our way to the tube at Southgate. For all home matches the Arsenal players met up at the Kings Cross Hotel, close by the station. Everyone had to be present by no later than 11.30 am.

We all enjoyed a light lunch of fish, or poached eggs on toast and then settled down for a final team briefing, leaving for the ground on the team coach at about 1.00 pm.

As we made our way closer to Highbury we could see lots of fans already making their way to the match. They were all in boisterous mood and looking forward to seeing their side in action against Liverpool.

I was sat on the bus next to Joe Mercer. The oldest and the youngest together. He had moved next to me deliberately so that he could help calm my nerves.

'Everyone on the bus has had to go through this to play in their first game,' he said. 'Don't worry about anything, just be yourself and do what comes naturally.'

The bus pulled up outside the main entrance and there were hundreds of supporters, young and old, waiting for us.

As each player got off the bus a few fans would rush forward for autographs. It was quite an experience to be treated in exactly the same way and I signed a few autograph books, papers and magazines before I was able to make my way with the other players into the stadium.

We went straight down to the dressing room and as I went in, once again there was my kit all set out below the number eight. Shorts, socks and a towel were neatly folded on the bench in front of my Arsenal shirt which was hanging from my peg. There were even clothes hangers waiting for our everyday gear.

I took my time getting ready, savouring every moment. Joe had told me not to rush things. As we were changing, Mr Whittaker came into the dressing room. He said: 'Go out there and do your best. Just remember it's 11 of us and 11 of them,' and then he came over to where I was sitting and quietly added, 'Listen to the older lads and you will be alright.'

Billy Milne was here, there and everywhere as various players wanted a massage or rub-down but I didn't need anything to get my blood pumping.

At last the time came to make our way outside. To get on the pitch you had to go down a couple of steps and as I came out into the open the noise from the supporters was deafening. I had never been in front of such a crowd before and it took my breath away.

As usual we had a little knockabout while the skippers tossed for ends and Arsenal started the match facing the big clock.

Once the game began I forgot all about the crowd. I seemed to be doing a lot of chasing around in the early minutes trying to find my feet as my team-mates became used to having me up front. Fortunately, most Arsenal first-teamers would watch the reserves playing at every opportunity so they had some idea of how I played.

Tommy Lawton began seeing a lot more of the ball and it wasn't long before he set up a few chances for me. From the first pass I was caught offside, the second one I snatched at too quickly and fired it over the bar, but the third pass put us one up after 20 minutes. Arthur Milton crossed from the right, Tommy rose to head it down in the penalty area, and as the ball came to me I went for goal. Although Liverpool keeper Dave Underwood got his foot to the ball, my shot had enough pace to cross the line. I had scored on my debut and the Arsenal supporters went wild.

Playing with Tommy was a treat. He would be talking to me all the time. 'I'll tell you where to go and when to be there,' he would say and he was nearly always right. As the ball came across into the middle he would call out 'Near post, far post, a flick on,' or whatever he intended to do. Nine times out of ten he did exactly what he said he would do. All I had to do was the running but that was my game anyway and I didn't mind doing that for Tommy as he let me bang the goals in. I only wished that I had played with him earlier in his career. He was still quick in short bursts, had a tremendous shot in either foot, and his heading was out of this world. I honestly believe that I could have been a better player if I had played more games with the great Tommy Lawton.

Sadly, all that euphoria from scoring a goal to put the Gunners ahead was to disappear six minutes later as tragedy struck.

Joe Mercer and our full back Joe Wade both went for the same ball, collided and a sickening crack could be heard all around the stadium. Joe Mercer's right leg had been fractured in two places below the knee and he left the field on a stretcher, never to play again. It was a heartbreaking moment for everyone concerned but it was especially hard for me as Joe had taken me under his wing and looked after me as I came to grips with being at such a big club as the Arsenal.

My friendship with the great man didn't end there though because every year Joe would send my wife and I Christmas cards and when my two daughters were born we received some beautiful presents from him. He was a very special man and I will never forget him.

There were no substitutes in those days so the ten men had to battle against the full might of a Liverpool side still smarting after going a goal down. Billy Liddell did some raiding down the wings while Geoff Twentyman made sure I knew he was about. But we caught them again on the break and Don Roper doubled the score just before half time. When the whistle went we headed straight for the dressing room with everyone wanting to know the full extent of Joe's injury, although deep down we all knew his leg had been broken.

Mr Whittaker came in soon after us and said that Joe was on his way to hospital but that he would want us to do our best to secure a victory. He then told us that he was pleased with our first half performance and that we had to keep playing the same way in the second half. Later he came over to me and congratulated me on my first goal in league football and I apologised to him for missing a couple of good opportunities.

Tommy was in fine form during the interval and I could see that he was going to turn it on in the second half.

When the match re-started, he was immediately into the action to set me up twice in quick succession but I missed a sitter with the first and then hit my shot into the side netting. Then Don Roper made a break down the wing and crossed, Tommy flicked it on into the penalty area and I dived to head past Underwood for my second goal. Tommy couldn't leave it at that. He tried everything going to put a hat-trick on a plate for me but I just couldn't put another one away.

When the game finished we ran off the pitch to a tremendous roar from the Arsenal fans. It was a moment that will stay with me forever. Poor Liverpool never recovered and ended the season relegated to Division Two after finishing in bottom place.

In the dressing room the realisation of Joe Mercer's injury kept celebrations down but Tommy came over to me and said 'That's the start of a good career, son.'

We all quietly made our way to the players lounge along the corridor where we had a cup of tea and a smoke. Smoking was not allowed in the dressing room.

For the first time in my life I was interviewed by reporters for the Sunday papers after the game. I was still in a state of shock and all I can remember was thanking Arsenal for giving me the opportunity and Tommy Lawton for giving me all those goalscoring chances.

The following Monday I made my way as usual to Highbury for training but I had not been in the dressing room for more than five minutes when Bert Owen popped his head round the door to say that I was wanted in Mr Whittaker's office.

I put my shirt and tie back on, tidied myself up and went up the stairs to where Miss Grosvenor was waiting. She opened the manager's door and I went in.

'I have some good news for you Derek,' he said. 'You have been selected in the Wales squad to play against Austria on the 9th of May.'

Mr Whittaker shook me by the hand but I was too overcome to say a word. It was the last thing I expected. I was flabbergasted, I made my way back to the dressing room but everything I did seemed to be in slow motion. I was nearly late for the start of training but the whole session seemed to pass by in a daze.

After training the lads all congratulated me on my selection and I made my way back home to the digs. I found out later that no Welsh selector had even seen me play. One of them rang Mr Whittaker and he recommended me for my first cap.

The first thing I did when I arrived home was go to the nearest public telephone box and called my sister Violet who was in Hammersmith Hospital where she was having a baby. Violet had moved to Willesden when she married and I wanted her to know the news straightaway. Vera, my eldest sister, lived in Oxford so they were both within easy distance of my digs if I was ever in need of anything. Violet had a baby girl, called Mary who is my goddaughter, but I don't think the news of my selection for Wales helped her with the birth in any way.

Then a stream of telegrams began to arrive, including one from mam and dad which I still treasure, and one from Barry Town. I was on cloud nine. Within 48 hours of making my Football League debut I had been included in the Wales squad. But then it became even better as I heard the radio give out the actual team to play against the Austrians and I was included at inside right, playing alongside the great Trevor Ford.

But there was still league football to be played and the Easter programme was very busy. After the Liverpool match we faced three games in just four days. On Good Friday, Portsmouth were the visitors to Highbury and I was delighted to see my name on the team-sheet when it was pinned up on Thursday after training. The only change was Peter Goring coming in for the unfortunate Joe Mercer who was still in the Royal Northern Hospital.

At the team talk, Mr Whittaker told us it would be a tough game, especially for me as I would be marked by England legend, Jimmy Dickinson.

When we returned to the digs that afternoon, Jack and I

went round the corner to a small snooker hall that was close by. We spent an hour or two in there with soft drinks – definitely no beer – and chatted about the heavy weekend programme about to start. Jack was used to it but I had never been involved in so many high profile games in such a short period. I just hoped that Mr Whittaker felt I was up to playing all these games in quick succession.

Good Friday came and we made our way to the hotel where we all met for lunch and a final briefing from Mr Whittaker and the older more experienced players.

I was told to just go out and have a go – which suited me as that is how I always liked to play. The bus to the ground was strangely quiet as we suddenly realised we were without Joe Mercer.

It was the same ritual as before. Sign a few autographs at the door before making our way to the dressing room. Throughout my career I always ensured I made time to sign autographs and have a chat with supporters as they are the people who paid our wages. As usual the kit was laid out ready for us. I always put my right boot on first, it's just one of those things. Some players have silly superstitions but if it helps them relax then it is worthwhile.

The match against Pompey couldn't have gone better. I managed to score another two goals in a 3-0 win and gave the experienced Jimmy Dickinson a bit of a run-around. I headed the first from close range and then beat Norman Uprichard, their keeper, with a crisp shot into the corner of the net. But just as against Liverpool, I missed a few chances and again I could have had a hat-trick with a little more composure in front of goal.

There was no time to relax at the end of the game. We were taken by bus to Euston Station and caught the overnight sleeper to Newcastle where we were playing on Easter Saturday. Some of the boys relaxed by playing cards on the train, others read books or magazines. I hated playing cards so I whiled away the time reading the papers and a couple of magazines. On arrival at Newcastle we were taken to a hotel for the night and it was straight to bed for everyone as we were all exhausted.

After a light breakfast we had some spare time to relax before travelling the ten minutes or so to St James' Park. Jack Kelsey had received an injury in the game against Portsmouth so Con Sullivan took over in goal for his league debut. I knew exactly how he felt.

The Magpies were an impressive team in those days. With players like Jackie Milburn and Bobby Mitchell up front they could always score goals and they had a wing half called Jimmy Scoular who rarely took any prisoners, as I was to find out soon enough.

We ran out on to the pitch and began warming-up by just knocking the ball about. In those days you didn't come out half an hour before the game to warm up. All we had was a little kick-about while the referee tossed up with the skippers.

I was standing on the edge of the area when I heard someone coming up behind me. It was Scoular.

'Are you the young laddie who's been scoring all the goals lately?' he said in his gruff Scottish accent. I told him that I had managed to net four times in the last two games.

He stared straight at me and replied 'Well let me tell you this sonny, the only kicks you are going to get today are the ones I'll be giving you,' and with that he turned and went back to his team-mates.

After believing that playing football at the top level was easy following those two victories against Liverpool and Portsmouth, Newcastle United – and Jimmy Scoular in particular – brought me straight back down to earth. Arthur Milton and Cliff Holton scored for us but the Magpies were too strong on the day and won 5-2. I would have liked to have taken note of Jackie Milburn in action but when you are playing you have to focus your mind on the job at hand. And my job was trying to score goals and still get off the pitch in one piece as Scoular was true to his word and gave me a severe kicking all over the park. I did manage a couple of shots on target but Ronnie Simpson was as safe as houses in the Newcastle goal.

The three games in a week had been very tiring as I had been doing all the running for Tommy Lawton. But it wasn't finished yet as we travelled straight back from Newcastle to prepare for the return game at Fratton Park against Portsmouth on Easter Monday.

Jack Kelsey was fit again and he came back in for Con Sullivan while Bill Dodgin was brought in to stiffen the defence at centre half.

Pompey were much better at home than they were at Highbury three days previously. I had very few chances on goal, perhaps I was missing the service from Tommy Lawton who had been dropped since the trip to Newcastle. I think Don Roper scored for us but the match ended in a 1-1 draw and everyone was pleased when the referee blew the final whistle. All those games in such a short time took their toll on us and it was a weary squad that made the trip home from Portsmouth that Easter Monday evening.

There was just enough time for a few of us to go to see Joe Mercer who was still in hospital. It was very upsetting seeing him lying there knowing that his career was over. Afterwards he would make a joke of the whole thing by saying that when his leg was broken he was more afraid of what our trainer Billy Milne would do to him than he was of the damage.

In the final game of the season against Middlesbrough I was a little too eager in the first half hour and caught offside time and time again but I kept plugging away. Then after half an hour I slipped a pass into Don Roper who opened the scoring but Lindy Delapenha equalised a little against the run of play to make it all square at half time. I took a bit of a buffeting from their keeper Rolando Ugolini during the second half but Doug Lishman headed in an Arthur Milton cross to put us back in the lead. Luckily, I managed a close range effort from a short Logie pass that took a slight deflection off Middlesbrough defender Derek Stonehouse for my fifth goal in five first team starts and we ended up 3-1 winners to round off the season with a deserved victory. To make things even better, I was given a rise of £1 for making the first team for those final few games of the season.

After being champions in 1952-53 the club had slipped to 12th place so we were all aware that it wasn't good enough for Arsenal Football Club. Now the season was over we all had to wait to see the retained list to find out if we were required for the following season. In those days there were no such things as two or three year contracts. Every player signed for a year and then waited to find out if they were wanted for another year. And of course we were all rather anxious and obviously very keen to find out the club's decision. Finally, a week or so after the end of the season a letter arrived at my digs from the club and in it I was offered another year's contract with a rise of £2, taking me up to £14 during the season. The letter also gave the date in July when I had to report back to Highbury for pre-season training. The Arsenal club generally finished the season with a short tour to the continent, usually Switzerland and Germany, but I had another trip on my mind as the international in Vienna was coming up.

6

ON THE
INTERNATIONAL STAGE

All the players at the club said their goodbyes for the summer and I headed back home to Barry. It was good to see all the family again although after sharing digs with Jack, it did seem very crowded back at home.

I had an anxious few days waiting for my passport to arrive and it was a relief when it finally dropped on the doormat. At last the day came when all the Welsh players had to report at the Royal Hotel in Cardiff. Everyone had to be there by Wednesday, 5 May, officials included. It's probably no surprise to learn that there were more officials than players making the trip. We called them 'The First Team' – because they were always first on the coach or plane wherever we went.

Although John Charles had been selected no one knew if he was going to make the trip. Leeds United had given permission for him to play at first but then went back on their word by saying that he was needed on their end of season tour to Holland. Derrick Sullivan of Cardiff City was put on standby in case Big John failed to arrive.

None of the officials said anything to us on arrival at the hotel where we stayed the night. The following morning a coach took us to London (Heathrow) Airport and following only a short delay we boarded the plane – after the selectors who had been first up the steps of course.

This was my first time in an aircraft and I can't say I really enjoyed it. I didn't like the feeling of being shut in but I sat next to Jack Kelsey and he kept me occupied while the plane took off. Just before it went down the runway we were brought boiled sweets to suck and cotton wool to put in our ears when the engines were at their loudest.

On arrival at Vienna Airport one of the Wales officials handed out forms to all the players. These turned out to be expenses sheets. Every player had to put down the cost of getting to Cardiff so they could be reimbursed. No first class travel was allowed. The amount had to be absolutely correct otherwise it would be thrown out.

Austria was very wet. It was torrential rain and it carried on all through Thursday and Friday putting a stop to any training. The only bright spot was the arrival of John Charles straight from his club's summer tour of Holland.

On the Saturday morning, the day before the game, we went to the Vienna Stadium for a light training session to get the feel of the place and loosen our muscles.

Later that day we went on a sight-seeing tour of the city which ended with a visit to the British Garrison stationed there.

Walley Barnes had been appointed Wales team manager as he was still unfit after not fully recovering from the knee injury he received in the FA Cup Final of 1952. Walley needed to be very diplomatic when a row broke out over the type of ball that would be used in the match. The Austrians wanted to play with a Swiss ball as that would be used in the 1954 World Cup which was being held in Berne. We really didn't mind what type of ball would be used but the Austrians refused to allow us the use of one for training. It took Walley some time to convince the Austrian officials to give us a couple of these new balls for a practice session.

We had another spell of training on the morning of the match, and then in no time at all we were out on the field and the national anthems were being played.

What a fantastic moment when you are representing your

country and you hear the national anthem being played. It really does bring tears to your eyes, I know it did mine and I suspect the same happened to Cliff Jones of Swansea Town who was also making his debut.

Austria were a strong side that had only recently been beaten 1-0 by Hungary who were reckoned to be Europe's best team at the time and the odds were in their favour to beat Wales. But they did have to make a change in goal where their regular keeper Tiger Zeman was injured and he was replaced by a lad called Pelikan. I had a chat with Trevor Ford about keepers when we knew of the change and we both decided that we would put as much pressure as possible on the new man. 'When we get in the penalty box I'll tee him up and you hit him,' said Fordy. That may sound drastic these days but at that time you could charge into keepers – remember Nat Lofthouse for Bolton Wanderers in the Cup Final although on the continent referees weren't quite so keen.

Charlo had one of his best games for Wales and we needed him because the Austrians were big and strong and they played some neat football before taking the lead. Chances at the other end were few and far between but on one occasion I did manage to go in on their keeper after a rare corner kick and he finished up caught in the netting at the back of the goal and hanging upside down. Perhaps he really was injured because he never came out for the second half, instead they put on a new keeper and also a new winger. Fordy and I looked at each other and silently agreed to welcome the new man in the best possible way. He went up for a cross and collided with the keeper, and as the Austrian came down clutching the ball I shoulder charged him. The crowd went mad and one of the big Austrian defenders raced over towards me with fists raised but the referee never blew up for anything and the game carried on. I can tell you that the tackles by their defenders were vigorous to say the least after that incident. Towards the end they scored another but it was a good showing against a powerful team.

Afterwards it was claimed that they had broken FIFA rules by using two substitutes but nothing came of it. The Austrian authorities suspended one of their players after the match for ripping Charlo's thigh open with his studs. Most of us carried the marks of unsporting challenges and I had a six-inch gash across my knee.

Linking up with Fordy was a fantastic experience and it was the start of a great friendship which lasted long after we both retired. We used to play golf together when our paths crossed. He was that mean he was the only man I know who could go up to a counter to buy 20 cigarettes and yet come back and open a packet that only had one left in it. Of course in those days almost everyone smoked. Even Ivor Allchurch used to enjoy a cigar after a match with a glass of wine.

In the evening there was a dinner for all the participants and then back to the hotel ready for an early start in the morning.

When we landed at London Airport we went to collect our luggage and one of the Welsh officials came around to give us our expenses, or in some cases, tell us we were wrong with the amount we had claimed. Every player who kept his international shirt was docked £1 and that was deducted from the expenses given to us.

There was no debriefing by anyone, the players just said their goodbyes and went in their own direction to get back home. I was going back to Barry so joined up with Fordy, Alf Sherwood, and the two Swansea lads, Ivor Allchurch and Cliff Jones who were all catching the South Wales train from Paddington.

It was back to training on my own at Jenner Park as I wanted to stay reasonably fit before going back to the Arsenal in the middle of July. The new season couldn't come quick enough for me but it would start with a real sting in the tail.

Incidentally, I wasn't the only Tapscott making a name in footballing circles. My brother David, who was a much better footballer than me as a youngster, had gone to Everton for a trial. He had been playing regularly for Barry Town and had obviously impressed their scouts. He did very well at Goodison Park and after the trial Everton were prepared to sign him on but when they went through his medical report they found out that he had glandular fever as a young lad and so they turned him down. Added to that, my sister Pat was in the Barry Ladies team.'

7

MY FIRST FULL SEASON

Back to Mrs Ring and the digs in Muswell Hill. It had been a good summer at home but I was keen to get on and make my mark at the Arsenal.

Every player was carefully weighed when he reported back but I never had any weight problems. In fact I could have done with putting on another couple of pounds as long as it didn't slow me up. Training started with roadwork which consisted of endless runs around the area surrounding Highbury. I enjoyed the running but some of the players weren't too keen although they knew it had to be done. Even the great Arsenal had no special training ground. Now and again we used an open area at Southgate which was very handy for me and Con Sullivan as it was quite close to our digs.

The club organised a couple of friendlies leading up to the start of the season. They were low-key affairs but you weren't allowed to slacken off. Leslie Compton and Alf Fields would make sure of that and no one would argue with them.

The final match on the last Saturday before the season's opener was always the first team against the reserves and it was played at Highbury usually in front of a full house. I was selected in the reserves and even though we were all Arsenal players, it was expected that everyone play as if it was a proper game. I managed to go in hard on a couple of the lads but never got a sniff of a goal.

The only absentees from the previous season were Joe Mercer and George Swindin who had decided to retire after Jack Kelsey had taken his place in goal.

The days leading up to the first match at home to Newcastle United were tense as we wondered who would be selected to start the season off. You can imagine my disappointment when I was left out of the line-up, particularly after finishing the previous season in the first team and winning a cap for Wales. Brian Walsh was at outside right with Jimmy Logie inside him and Cliff Holton led the line.

Brian was a super fellow and we exchanged Christmas cards for many years until he passed away recently. A member of his family rang me up to let me know the sad news. Brian, who was a fully trained accountant, used to go to night school to continue his studies even though he was playing for Arsenal. On the field he was one of the quickest players I have ever seen and I believe he was a sprint champion in his younger days. He could beat his man with pace and send over an accurate cross and I really enjoyed playing with him. At Arsenal he was known affectionately as 'Daisy' and in September 1955 he was involved in one of the strangest deals ever. Cardiff City transferred their two outside rights, Mike Tiddy and Gordon Nutt to Arsenal in exchange for a cash payment and Brian Walsh. I know who had the best of that deal.

It was a poor opener to the season with Newcastle winning 3-1 and I hoped that my chance would come in the next match when we visited Everton. Sure enough Mr Whittaker decided on a number of changes and Dennis Evans and Peter Goring came into the defence and Jimmy Bloomfield and Joe Haverty made their debuts on the flanks. I was at number ten in place of Doug Lishman.

It was a much improved performance but the match still ended in a defeat. We were at the Hawthorns three days later to face West Brom and that was the first time I played in Division One with Brian Walsh. I had been switched to inside right and Tommy Lawton was at centre forward but once again we were well-beaten to make it three defeats from our opening three matches.

It wasn't until the seventh match of the season that I broke my duck. We beat Sheffield United 4-0 and I netted one along with Doug Lishman who was scoring goals for fun even though the results were poor. I managed another at Maine Road in the next match against Bert Trautmann but Manchester City won 2-1.

But I was given a tonic when a letter arrived for me at the club. It was from the Football Association of Wales telling me I had been selected to play against Yugoslavia in Cardiff on 22 September.

Before that match however we had to travel to Deepdale where the 'Preston Plumber', Tom Finney, put on the style to beat us 3-1. That was six defeats from our opening nine games and we were way down the Division One table.

We stayed in Preston for the night before travelling back on the Sunday. Arsenal were a club that really looked after their players. After a relaxing day I joined up with Jack Kelsey, Dave Bowen and Walley Barnes at Paddington Station and we all came down to Cardiff by train to meet up with the rest of the lads at the Royal Hotel. This was the first time in Arsenal's history that they had four players selected in the same Wales side. Just as for my first cap, the expenses sheets were handed out before any discussions on tactics. Walley decided on the way we would play which we readily accepted as he was the most experienced player in the squad. But this match cost me almost all my £10 fee for playing as I had to buy tickets for all the family and the Welsh FA were known to be fairly slow at giving out complimentaries.

We knew very little about the Yugoslavs, there being no pen pictures or information available like there is today. On the day of the game we did a little light training in the morning, had lunch of fish, chicken or poached eggs, and then relaxed in the afternoon. Most of us would go up to our rooms and lie on our beds and perhaps read for a little, but some of the lads played cards. At 5.00 pm we boarded the coach for Ninian Park.

The game itself was poor quality. They were harder and stronger than we were and they won comfortably 3-1. I was once again at inside right with Fordy down the middle but the outside left was Roy Clarke of Manchester City who had regained his place from Cliff Jones. Roy Paul of Manchester City was at right half. Roy was quite a character and a bit of a wine buff. He was very fond of a glass or two. Fordy gave away loads of free kicks as the Dutch referee Leo Horn didn't seem to like the physical side of the game and then Roy conceded a penalty which really got them going. He trapped the ball but it bounced up and hit him on the arm. Nine times out of ten a referee would have waved play on but not this one. Their substitute scored from the spot and added two other goals late on. At the after-match banquet, Billy Reed, our outside right from Ipswich Town, collapsed and was taken to St David's Hospital where he was kept overnight, but fortunately he soon recovered. He had been injured during the game but must have suffered from the after-effects of concussion.

We said our goodbyes the following day knowing that in three weeks we would be meeting again as the visit of Scotland was next on the fixture list, but for me and the other Arsenal lads there was an international adventure of a different sort on the horizon.

When we returned to Highbury the following week all the players were asked to attend a special team meeting. When we were all present, Mr Whittaker told us that the club had agreed to go to Russia to play against the famous Moscow Dynamo. Unfortunately, the Football League would not allow us to postpone the matches either side of the trip so it was going to be a very hectic time.

Tommy Lawton was recalled for the games against

Burnley and at Leicester and this time I was able to help him score twice in successive matches.

We went to Leicester by coach because straight after the match we would be staying in the Coburg Court Hotel in Bayswater before flying out to Moscow early the following morning.

The party was split into two groups. When Arsenal travelled abroad they always arranged the transport so that the players were split up. So in party one, which was my group, we had a goalkeeper, two full backs and so on, while travelling in a second plane was a similar assortment of players. Tommy Lawton, Walley Barnes, Don Roper, Jack Kelsey, Bill Dickson and Tom Whittaker were all in my group along with Raymond Glendenning the commentator and journalist. I believe this arrangement had been going since the Torino club lost nearly all its players in a plane crash a few years previously. Stanley Rous was amongst the officials travelling in our plane.

Each player was given a small booklet with all the arrangements and timings listed in it. We were even reminded to put our watches back an hour as BST ended later that evening. We were also told in no uncertain terms that every player was expected to be in their rooms well before midnight, but with such an early start in the morning, that suited us all anyway.

The coach arrived for my group at 7.00 am and we left for Northolt Airport, which was near Uxbridge. As we boarded the coach we were handed our passports and visas which the Russian authorities had left to the last minute before returning. Not everyone had been granted visas as I seem to remember that a group of fans were left behind as well as a few journalists. Our plane left for Prague at 8.30 am with a re-fuelling stop in Frankfurt. The second plane followed on 15 minutes later.

We had the fuel stop in Frankfurt which gave us the

chance to stretch our legs for an hour and then we were off again.

When we approached Prague we were escorted down by Russian MIG fighters until we landed safely. The British planes were then given only half an hour to offload and refuel before heading back to London leaving us to board a couple of Russian Aeroflot planes for the flight on to Moscow. As soon as we boarded we realised the luxury we had been flying in compared to the Russian planes. They were much older and had probably seen war service. It was very cold inside, so no heating, and there were no safety belts. We had already been travelling 11 hours and most of us could have done with a snack and at the very least a cup of tea but we were told that there would be refreshments on board during the flight to Moscow.

Refreshments duly arrived but all we were given was cold tea or coffee and some rock-hard biscuits. After about three hours in the air, we started descending and thought at last we had arrived in Moscow but no, we landed in Warsaw for another refuelling stop. This time we were again allowed out but all the shops in the airport were shut so we still couldn't get anything to eat or drink. In any case we did not have any foreign money as none had been given to us.

Back in the air for another two hours but as we approached the Russian capital the weather deteriorated and because of the dense fog we were forced to travel on to Minsk.

All the careful arrangements made by the club went out of the window as we now found ourselves landing in Minsk, nowhere near our designated hotel in Moscow. To our surprise the second plane, which took off after us, was already on the tarmac at Minsk.

We were put up in what I can only describe as a dormitory building although it was classed as a hotel. A big room with 20 or 30 beds was made available for us and we spent an uncomfortable hour or two with hardly anyone getting any sleep. We were given chicken soup before we left the airport but I don't think anyone could eat it. Tommy Lawton pulled out a strange looking piece of meat from his soup and it put everyone else off eating theirs. Then just as we were settling down in the communal dormitory we were woken up to get ready for the return to the airport and the onward journey. Washing facilities were primitive to say the least and we looked a very ragged and untidy bunch as we took our places back on the plane.

Before leaving, a breakfast was served consisting of boiled eggs and toast but they were both so hard that you couldn't eat either of them. The coffee was so strong that you couldn't drink it so most of the lads, including me, went without anything at all.

We hoped there would be some refreshments available on the two hour flight from Minsk to Moscow but nothing was offered to us.

When we arrived at Moscow Airport we were kept in passport control for another two hours before being allowed through to a big hall where a welcoming party gave us bouquets of flowers. Then we had to stand and listen to speeches before boarding a coach which took us to the Hotel Sovetskaya in the centre of Moscow.

The hotel was just what we had expected an old Russian building to be like, ornate high ceilings and a huge entrance hall. It was a fabulous hotel, spotlessly clean but we couldn't stay long to admire the décor as we had to leave our luggage in our rooms and go off for some gentle loosening up. I was rooming with Bill Dickson and before we left for training he opened the windows for some fresh air. When we got back we found someone had padlocked the windows shut – for security reasons we were told.

It was windy and raining as we made our way by coach to the Dynamo Stadium. The inside of the stadium was magnificent, even better than Highbury. The dressing room floor was carpeted and there were big couches and easy chairs to relax in.

Unfortunately, the pitch did not match up to the surroundings as the grass was long and the rain made the ground very heavy to play on. On one side of the stadium were two huge banners of Stalin and Lenin that overshadowed everything else.

After the training session we returned to the hotel for a light meal. We had a few hours spare time so some of the lads made their way to the entrance to go outside but they were stopped at the door by a couple of soldiers with guns.

In the evening we were allowed out but the whole party had to go together, no one was allowed to stay on their own in the hotel, or go out on their own. We just stretched our legs walking the streets around the hotel.

After a restful night, we had breakfast and went to the stadium for a light training session. In the afternoon we rested up until it was time to board the coach in readiness for the game.

The match itself, played under the Dynamo floodlights on 5 October, was a good standard but we didn't do ourselves justice because we were all tired out and hadn't recovered from the travelling. We held them out until just before the interval but they took us apart in the second half to win 5-0 and they even missed a penalty. That was one game where I really wanted to score as in goals for Dynamo was the great Russian international, Lev Yashin.

Slightly unnerving were the lady cleaners who were in the dressing rooms all the time we were in there, even when we were changing. They were sweeping and cleaning up all around us and were even in the baths and shower areas keeping everything clean. Like most things abroad, you accept it and just get on with whatever you are doing.

The following day was Tommy Lawton's 35th birthday and

the Moscow Dynamo club provided a celebratory lunch consisting of caviar, steaks and a huge chocolate birthday cake which we all helped finish off in double quick time.

After that we were taken on a sight-seeing tour of Moscow which included a trip on their Underground system. That was a strange sight because there were no advertisements on the tiled walls like there is in London, and certainly no graffiti. Once again there were cleaners everywhere making sure the place was kept in a spotless condition.

We visited the Kremlin – no cameras allowed in certain areas there – Lenin's tomb and all the other famous sights and we also enjoyed a look around the famous GUM department store. Most of us bought cameras as they seemed to be the best buy, but everything you could think of was available there.

When it was time to leave the hotel there was another small hold up while we waited for our passports and visas to be returned to us but we eventually made our way to the airport to start the long trek back to London.

When we eventually arrived home we were disappointed to learn that the papers had been hammering us for our performance against the Russians. Little did they know of the difficulties we had to overcome with all the travelling problems. It was no secret that most of us were browned off by the trip but that licking from the critics was harder to bear than the tiredness we suffered.

For some of the older and more travelled Arsenal players it was just another fixture but for me it was a wonderful and rather bewildering experience to visit a place which previously was just a spot on the map. I learned a lot from Dynamos' methods. For instance, the way they got rid of the ball quickly, and the speedy manner they fell back into defence after putting in an all-out attack with the two half backs in close support. The charging of the goalkeeper however is one thing that always seemed to cause me problems. We understood in the British game that it was perfectly legal yet the first time I barged the Dynamo keeper as he held on to the ball I was penalised. There should have been one international ruling as it caused me problems throughout my international career.

Three days later it was back to normal in the league and we were in Hillsborough facing Sheffield Wednesday. Brian Walsh came in at outside right and I moved inside. Goals from Don Roper and Jimmy Bloomfield, his first in the league, gave us a 2-1 victory and we were back to the bread and butter of Division One football.

I was delighted to receive another letter from the Football Association of Wales telling me that I was selected to play against Scotland in Cardiff on 16 September.

As Jack Kelsey, Walley Barnes and Dave Bowen also received letters, this meant that Arsenal would have to make at least four changes for the match against Portsmouth at Highbury. In those days you couldn't cancel a league match no matter how many of your players were absent on international duty. Those changes were too much for the club to overcome and Pompey won 1-0.

I was also very pleased to receive another letter, this one was from Glenys Laban in Barry inviting me to her 21st birthday party on the evening of the Scotland match. I quickly replied that all things being favourable, I would make it to Barry after the reception following the game.

The side to play the Scots was unchanged from the Yugoslavia match so it was good to know that Billy Reed had no lasting effects from his collapse after the previous game. I travelled down to Cardiff with my Arsenal team-mates and as usual we all met up at the Royal Hotel where the 'First Team' were already settled and enjoying full use of all the facilities.

George Young skippered Scotland and Tommy Docherty was at wing half. It looked as though it was going to end in a

0-0 draw until Pat Buckley scored the winner for them in the closing stages. So my first three caps all ended in defeat and I was still waiting for my first international goal. England were our next opponents at Wembley Stadium in October but I wondered whether I had done enough to keep my place.

I attended the after-match reception with one eye on the clock, and it was quite late when I arrived in Barry for the final stages of Glen's birthday party but we still had a good time during what was left of the evening.

Back to Highbury for the start of the week's training and I was having a problem holding on to my position in the first team. Although I missed the next match against Aston Villa I was back in for the visit of Sunderland.

In those days the north-easterners were a good strong side and in Len Shackleton they had one of the finest inside forwards to play the game. He certainly turned on the style in front of a full house at Highbury but we did suffer from a couple of injuries. Arthur Milton was hurt after a challenge and I was pushed out to the wing to try and provide some service for Cliff Holton. For some reason I couldn't control the ball at all and was sending crosses all over the place, usually high and wide behind the Sunderland goal. When play was held up for another stoppage Shack, who had the ball at his feet, came over to where I was standing. 'What's the matter with you today, Tappy?' he said. 'You're not hitting the ball correctly. Look, get round the ball when you strike it with the inside of your foot and it will curl wherever you want it to go.' He then showed me where to put my foot on the ball. 'Keep practising and you will see the benefit.' It was incredible that a man of his standing would be prepared to offer advice to a young player like me who wasn't even on his side. Shack was a real gentleman and it was criminal that he only won a few caps for England. In the short time available his advice made little difference however and we were well-beaten 3-1.

When we came off the pitch at the end of the game he came over to shake my hand and said that I had done a little better in the second half. Less than two weeks later our paths were to cross again.

I was delighted when my letter calling me to play against England arrived and I was very excited at the prospect of making my first trip to Wembley Stadium.

Johnny King of Swansea was winning his first cap in goal in place of the injured Jack Kelsey and Stuart Williams was at right back for Walley Barnes who had still not fully recovered from that 1952 Cup Final injury. The big change was up front where John Charles was selected alongside Trevor Ford and Ivor Allchurch. I was on the right wing with Roy Clarke on the other flank.

Lining up for England was an impressive array of talent with Roger Byrne at left back opposing me while Bill Slater of Wolves was at left half. Luckily for us Nat Lofthouse was injured so Ronnie Allen of West Brom switched from the left wing to centre forward and Frank Blunstone of Chelsea came in for his debut.

We trained at the Vickers Works in Weybridge and devised a couple of good moves but injuries would turn out to cost us dearly.

As both sides lined up in the tunnel I found myself opposite Stanley Matthews as we were both number sevens. He asked me if it was my first time at Wembley and I told him it was. 'Go out and play your normal game and you will be alright,' he said.

That was the start of a friendship with the great man that lasted throughout our careers. Whenever Blackpool played Arsenal at Bloomfield Road I would give Stan any complimentary tickets I could get hold of. When he came to Highbury he would do the same for me. Stan was a superb player. Every full back tried to kick him off the park but he was too good for most players. The only defender I knew who could usually get the better of Stan was Alf Sherwood of Cardiff City and Wales.

Just before we walked down the tunnel, Len Shackleton came up and asked Stan if he could have a few words with me. Stan obliged by moving back a place leaving Shack standing opposite me. He said, 'What I told you the other week was for your own good, I didn't mean it to be bigheaded in any way. If you keep practising it will do wonders for your career.' Shack was a real gentleman with a great personality. Everyone knew he was like that, and what an inside forward. He could almost make the ball talk. He was one of the best players in the country yet his face didn't fit with the powers-that-be and that is why he only ever won a few caps.

John Charles put us ahead late in the first half and with Ivor Allchurch at his brilliant best, it looked as though we had a good chance of beating England. Then disaster struck as first Derrick Sullivan was stretchered off and then Ray Daniel collapsed and was helped off to leave us down to nine men. Although they came back in the second half, Derrick was just a passenger on the wing and Ray, who had five stitches inserted in a head wound, had one eye closed. We held out until midway through the second half then Stan Matthews began to weave his magic and Chelsea's Roy Bentley headed his centre home to equalise. That was quickly followed by another from Bentley but Big John stormed through the middle to equalise. With just a few minutes left, Bentley scored again to claim a hat-trick and we were beaten 3-2.

Back at Arsenal we went on a depressing run of eight league games without a win but I scored in a 2-2 draw at Blackpool, who included both Matthews and Mortensen, and then kept my place to the end of the season.

On Christmas Day I scored the only goal as we beat

Chelsea at Highbury and then two days later I netted again in a 1-1 draw at Stamford Bridge. On New Year's Day we drew 2-2 with West Brom at Highbury and I helped Tommy Lawton to a well-deserved goal. Things were starting to happen for me during that spell as Tommy had been re-instated in the team and I was suddenly getting goalscoring opportunities once again. In the third round of the FA Cup we were drawn at home to Cardiff City and we knew they would give us a good game. Our training was different for cup matches. The club would take us to a big hotel in Broadstairs, Kent from the Sunday to the Thursday just to change the routine. Wednesday mornings were either training or golf, so that was my first introduction to the game of golf.

I had been looking forward to the Cardiff match for some time as I had never forgotten that they had reckoned I was not good enough for them when I was still at Barry Town. I still have the programme for the game so can easily recall the teams.

We fielded Jack Kelsey; Walley Barnes, Dennis Evans; Peter Goring, Jim Fotheringham, Dave Bowen; Arthur Milton, Derek Tapscott, Tommy Lawton, Doug Lishman and Joe Haverty. As we expected it was a hard match but we went through thanks to a well-taken goal from Tommy. The Cardiff line-up that day was Ron Howells; Charlie Rutter, Alf Sherwood; Islwyn Jones, Stan Montgomery, Alan Harrington; Mike Tiddy, Cliff Nugent, Trevor Ford, Ron Stockin and Tommy Northcott.

Tommy Lawton gave Stan Montgomery a difficult afternoon but Monty close-marked him very well as he had played against him in Division Two and Three (South) and knew what to expect from the great man. It was good to play against my Welsh team-mates, Alf Sherwood and Trevor Ford and little did I know that Mike Tiddy would soon become an Arsenal colleague of mine. After the game I caught the train home to South Wales from Paddington with the City boys and met up with them in the Buffet car. Monty was still mad that Tommy had slipped him only once in the match and it ended with the winner.

He moaned, 'He only had one kick all game and still he scored.'

I told him that all it takes is one kick. He wasn't amused. When I returned to live in Cardiff I used to see Monty occasionally. He would always greet me with the words 'I know, one touch is enough.'

One week after beating City we were at White Hart Lane playing our fierce local rivals, Spurs. Only four or five matches were played that day because of heavy snow and we were lucky we didn't have to travel very far. Before the game started all they did was clear the lines and we played on a bed of snow.

Ted Ditchburn was their keeper and he was as hard as nails. At one point he caught the ball and I rushed in, as I usually did on keepers, to give him a good old-fashioned shoulder charge. Unfortunately, he seemed to be made of iron and I rebounded about five yards and fell to the ground. Ted cleared the ball upfield and then came over and picked me up saying, 'Tappy, I'm too big for you,' and he was right. They had other great players like Danny Blanchflower, Len Duquemin and Eddie Baily. If you needed a skipper at anything, not just football, Danny was your man. He was brilliant at getting the best out of his players and I am very proud of the special occasion I played under him in a representative match that I will tell you about later on. Eddie Baily was not very big but he was a brilliant footballer. He was another who could almost make the ball talk, while 'The Duke', Len Duquemin, was a good old-fashioned bustler of a centre forward. Anyway, I had the last laugh on iron man Ted Ditchburn as Tommy Lawton nicked a winner for us to send our fans home happy. We met up with most of the

Spurs lads in the players lounge after the game and I had a long chat with Danny. He was a softly-spoken man and very knowledgeable about the game even then. I was surprised that he never went on to become a top class manager when his playing career ended. One Spurs player who did of course was full back Alf Ramsey who ended up as England's manager when they won the World Cup in 1966. In those days though Alf was a totally different person and he must have worked really hard to end up with such a different personality just a few short years later.

After Spurs, Preston were the visitors to Highbury. We beat them 2-0, I scored one of the goals, but Mr Whittaker was a little unhappy about one aspect of my performance. 'I am delighted with your positional play and endeavour Derek,' he said, 'but you sometimes spoil it by being off-balance and falling over too often. I believe we can solve the problem in the gym so it will mean some extra work for you.' I had never really thought about it but true to his word, he had me in the gym over the next few weeks twisting and turning and learning how to keep my balance. I don't really think it made any difference but who knows, if it helped me score even one more goal it was worth all the extra effort I put in.

Our cup victory over Cardiff meant nothing when we were beaten 1-0 at Molineux by Wolves in the next round. We bounced straight back from that reverse with the win over Preston. Tom Finney was out injured but Tommy Docherty more than made up for him with a super display at wing half. I almost scored in the first minute but Willie Cunningham got in the way and was knocked out. Then the 'Doc' was led off the field with blood streaming from a face wound and while he was receiving attention I opened the scoring. Doug Lishman moved down the right to pick up a pass from Don Roper and when his cross came in, I lifted it over George Thompson's head and into the net.

Cunningham was in the wars again before the end but with half backs Docherty and Forbes in fine form for the visitors it wasn't until the final few minutes that we settled the match. I had changed places with winger Don Roper and slipped a pass to him in the inside right position. With just the keeper to beat he belted the ball in from just outside the area.

I finally achieved what I had been hoping and working for on 26 February 1955 in my first full season with the Arsenal when Sheffield Wednesday came to town. It was a day when snow covered the pitch with only the lines having been cleared.

They had a lot of good players but none better than golden boy, Albert Quixall. As soon as the game started he began spraying passes all over the field. Jackie Sewell, a former team-mate of Tommy Lawton at Notts County was the other inside forward and he began looking dangerous as well, but big Jim Fotheringham was in good form at the heart of the Arsenal defence. We had changed our tactics slightly and Don Roper, although with number nine on his back, played a deep-lying role similar to the style of Don Revie and I don't think Don McEvoy, the Wednesday centre half, knew whether to follow him or keep up with me. I opened the scoring midway through the first half with an angled shot on the turn that beat Wednesday keeper Dave McIntosh. Danny Clapton, who had a good game that day in only his second first team start, provided the pass. Ten minutes later I doubled the score when I dashed through the middle chasing a Jack Kelsey goal kick. As McEvoy came across to stop me I glided past him and when McIntosh came out to meet me I slipped the ball into the corner of the net.

At half time we were 2-0 up and coasting. It all went haywire in the second half as first Jackie Marriott pulled one back from close in and then Quixall scored with a neat little header from an Alan Finney corner to level things up. It looked as though we had thrown away a point because I had missed some easy chances but then Peter Goring laid the ball back to me and I volleyed an unstoppable shot into the corner of the net for the winner and my first hat-trick in league football. It was a sweet moment for me and one that I will never forget.

Danny Clapton was a lovely young man. We were on our own in the dressing room one day when he told me that as a youngster he had developed meningitis and missed many months of schooling. As a result of the illness he also missed doing his national service. At one time he thought he would never play football again but here he was in the Arsenal first team.

Another match I won't forget in a hurry is our visit to Roker Park to play Sunderland. The good news for us was the absence of Len Shackleton who had been injured in a previous game and was having a run-out with their reserves although it would have been good to meet up with him again. It was a March day and bitterly cold when the match started yet the sun was shining brightly. The weather soon deteriorated and sleet showers changed to heavy snow. Soon after the start I went in for a ball with Sunderland's left back Joe McDonald and we clashed heads. I had treatment on the pitch but Joe had to go to the dressing room with a pad over his face to stop the flow of blood and it was some time before he returned. I only had a small cut to the side of my head but the collision left me with a blinding headache. I can't remember very much about the match after that and the referee had to stop the game several times for me to receive attention. The snow was driving down so heavily that the groundsmen had to keep clearing the touchlines with brooms. Somehow we managed to score through Jimmy Bloomfield and won the game 1-0. Playing for Sunderland in that game was Ken Chisholm who was a former Cardiff City inside forward who had been such an influence for the club when they won promotion to Division One in 1952.

The Easter period that season included two more matches against the Bluebirds so I asked Glen if she would like to come up to London to watch the game on Good Friday, followed by the visit of Blackpool on Easter Saturday. with the return at Ninian Park coming of course on the Bank Holiday Monday. I was delighted when she said that she would come and so arranged for her to stay with the daughter of my landlady, Mrs Ring.

Before she came however, I had some very special shopping to do.

I met Glen at Paddington and we travelled back to the digs where Mrs Ring and her daughter were waiting for us. After she had settled in we went for a short walk around the neighbourhood but I couldn't stay out long because of the match the following day.

On match day, Good Friday, Glen and I caught the 212 single decker bus from Muswell Hill which would take us close to Highbury. As she sat there looking out of the window I said 'You had better have this now in case I lose it,' and I handed her an engagement ring. I was the happiest man in the world when she accepted it but she did say straightaway that she was too young to get married. I hadn't really thought of the next stage, marriage, I was so caught up in the excitement of getting engaged. We decided that perhaps we would wait a year but then I thought that could be expensive. It was costing me £2 10s (£2.50) every other weekend for train fares back to Barry so I suggested that we arrange a date much sooner. I was quite lucky with the travelling really because I could usually get a lift from Highbury to Paddington Station with Dai Rees who at that time was the golf professional at South Herts Golf Club. Dai's parents lived in Barry but for some reason I was only given a lift to Paddington, not all the way to Barry.

I quite fancied getting married over Christmas but of

course that was out of the question because of matches over the holiday period. Neither of us wanted our big day to be midweek when many friends and relatives may not be able to come so, before the 212 bus had reached our destination, we decided that I would find out the dates of the tour Arsenal had already arranged for the summer and we could plan the wedding for as soon after that as possible.

Glen had a ticket in the stand with the other Arsenal ladies and I went into the dressing room where I told the lads of the good news before preparing for the game.

It turned out to be one of the best Easters ever because we beat City 2-0 and I scored both goals. The following day Matthews and Mortensen were in the Blackpool side beaten 3-0, and then we won the return at Ninian Park in Cardiff, 2-1 to make it an unbeaten and unbelievable weekend. The club gave me permission to travel back to Cardiff on the Sunday with Glen as I had to see her parents, and then tell mine of the good news. Naturally I was a little nervous at speaking to Glen's father but he soon put me at ease and wished us well.

Then it was on to Queen Street and my family and they were all excited at the news. My mam and sisters had known Glen for some time as she used to go to Jenner Park to watch Barry play and was always included in our group.

The victory over Cardiff was our last success of the season and we finished on a sour note with three defeats and a draw from our last four matches to end the campaign in ninth place, at least it was a little improvement on the previous year.

I played in 37 league games and scored 13 goals to finish up as third top scorer behind Dougie Lishman who got 19, and the 17 from Don Roper.

There was another international to play however and this time it meant my first trip to Belfast to play against Northern Ireland. The only change in the forward line from the last match against England at Wembley was Ivor Allchurch's brother Len coming in on the left wing for Roy Clarke, while Mel Charles, John's brother, made his debut at right half. We trained on Bangor's pitch as it was rock-hard just like Windsor Park where we would be playing the Irish. They had some good players in their line-up including an old foe of mine, Norman Uprichard of Portsmouth in goals. Danny Blanchflower captained the team from right half, Billy Bingham of Sunderland was on the right wing and Peter McParland of Aston Villa was at outside left.

This turned out to be another super show from Big John. Within the opening quarter of an hour he had scored twice. The first came from a Trevor Ford cross, and the second was after a typical barnstorming run down the middle. But the Irish never give up, particularly on their own soil and by half time they had levelled it at 2-2. Jack Kelsey was injured in the second half but recovered enough to continue playing. Charlo then netted his hat-trick when he climbed high with Uprichard who dropped the ball under the pressure, leaving an easy tap in for the winning goal. At last I had an international victory.

The wedding date had finally been arranged for 9 July but before that I had to undertake a tour of Switzerland and Germany with Arsenal. Barry Town had also been in touch with me to ask whether I would be interested in going on their trip to Sweden to play a few games. I quite fancied that but Arsenal flatly refused to give me permission. This was just as well because it would have meant postponing the wedding for a week or so. Glen sorted out all the arrangements for the big day, the church, reception, the invitations, cake and everything else that is needed. All I had to do was select a best man and I decided on Con Sullivan, who would soon be looking for someone else to share his digs when I left to start married life.

I did organise the honeymoon, or rather Miss Grosvenor

did. We had decided to go to Jersey and the club booked the flights and hotel for us although of course I paid the bills.

While Glen was making those arrangements, I flew out with the lads to Geneva where we were to play Grasshoppers on 11 May. That was a typically friendly encounter that finished 5-5 with Don Roper scoring a hat trick and Alex Forbes the other two. Four days later we played Young Boys of Berne and won 3-0 and I came on as a halftime replacement for young David Herd. The final match was in Germany against Munich 1860 and I struck both goals in the first half for a 2-1 victory.

We returned to England two days later to find that a number of us had received requests to play in testimonials all over the country. I thought I had a little time to spare and so agreed to put in appearances at some of them.

Time seemed to pass very quickly and I suddenly remembered that I had not even been in for a fitting for the suit I had ordered in Barry. With just two weeks to go before my big day I hurried back to Wales, visited the tailor, and then worried over whether I had given him enough time to make my suit. As it happened I had, and on the big day itself, I arrived at St Mary's Church, Barry Dock and sat waiting with best man Con for my bride to show up. She was well worth waiting for and I was the happiest man in the world when the vicar made us man and wife.

The reception was in the Barry Dock Hotel and it all went very well. We left early during the evening for Rhoose (Cardiff) Airport to catch the flight to Jersey for our honeymoon.

We couldn't get away from football even then. There were two lads from Barry on the plane and they knew who I was. When we reached our hotel, the Mount Millais in St Helier, there was an Arsenal supporter from Richmond already staying there. But we managed to keep it secret that we had only just been married until the last day or so when it finally came out. The hotel owners came from Maesteg and they made sure we had a very happy stay during our week there.

In next to no time we were boarding an early morning flight back to Heathrow. It was so early that the tube trains had still not started and we had to sit in the airport waiting for everything to open up.

Arsenal had found us a furnished flat in Turnpike Lane, actually nearer the Spurs ground than Highbury, so we had decided that it was easier to go directly to London rather than fly to Wales and then travel down on the train. Unfortunately the best laid plans sometimes do go astray and when we eventually arrived at the flat we found that all our belongings from Barry had failed to arrive. We had no clothes other than those we took on holiday, no bedding and no cutlery. Not the sort of start to married life that you would want. The only thing to do was go and see my former landlady Mrs Ring in Muswell Hill. She was as good as gold and gave us a meal and somewhere to rest while we chased up the whereabouts of our belongings.

We spent the night back in Turnpike Lane and on the Monday morning Glen and I went to Highbury. Mr Whittaker called us up to his office, congratulated us on our marriage, and gave us a cheque for £25. I changed the cheque for cash in the club office and when we left Highbury we bought a radio out of some of the money.

We still had a problem with our belongings which we had now established were still in Barry so I decided that the only course of action was to go and get them ourselves.

We went to see Dave Williams, a fanatical Arsenal supporter who had a car business not far from the ground. He loaned us a Morris 1000 and all I had to pay him was £1 for insurance. I told him that I had a driving licence but while that was true I had never driven a car in my life. I learnt to drive big trucks in the army – that's where I got my licence. Dave was very good to us and we kept in touch for many years after that.

We drove to Wales on the Tuesday, and in those days it was a long trip of eight or nine hours, collected our belongings, and then drove straight back because on the Wednesday I had to report to Highbury for pre-season training. For Glen it was a big change in her life. She used to work for a firm of accountants back home in Barry and now she was living in London and staying all alone in the flat while I went to work. After training on Wednesday we went to Woolworths to buy cutlery and one or two other items that we found we couldn't do without.

8

TAKING STOCK AND SCORING GOALS

Life was still the same when I went back to work even though I was now a married man. The training was just as difficult but at least I now had my own flat and Glen was there when I went home.

The season started with a tough opener at Blackpool where Matthews and Mortensen reigned supreme. I met up with Stan Matthews and gave him the complimentary tickets I had managed to get hold of as usual. But he didn't do me any favours in return and Blackpool won 3-1 although I did manage to get off the mark with our goal. It was Tommy Lawton who set the season alight in our next match by scoring a hat-trick against Cardiff City in a 3-1 win at Highbury. I had been looking forward to this meeting ever since I saw the 1955-56 fixtures but I was disappointed that injuries to my Wales colleagues, Alf Sherwood and Trevor Ford, meant that they were missing from the Bluebirds line-up. A former Wolves inside forward, Ron Stockin scored their goal but in truth we gave them a really good stuffing.

For the match at Burnden Park against Nat Lofthouse's Bolton Wanderers, Mr Whittaker had the idea of switching me to outside left to allow the inclusion of David Herd at number eight. We were roasted 4-1 and he came up to me after the match and said 'I now know a position where you will never be selected to play for Arsenal Football Club again.'

Sadly, though I didn't know it at the time, the goal Tommy Lawton scored that day would be his last for the Arsenal in Division One. By the end of the year he had left to join non-league side Kettering as player-manager. I missed him a great deal as he was good to be with both around the ground and during matches.

On 13 September, Arsenal played a representative match against an England Amateur XI. Amongst the array of amateur talent on show were Alec Jeffrey of Doncaster Rovers and one of the most famous of all England's amateur internationals, Bob Hardisty of Bishop Auckland. Mike Pinner of Cambridge University was in goals and he would later play for Arsenal, while I played up front for the Gunners.

Mr Whittaker was not in the best of health at this time and it was later in September that he completed the unusual deal with Cardiff that brought Mike Tiddy and Gordon Nutt to London while my old pal Brian Walsh, who had just made a return to the first team, made the opposite journey to Wales. Neither Tiddy nor Nutt had been in the Cardiff side beaten 3-1 just a few weeks earlier.

After that Cardiff victory we went seven games without a win although we did manage to draw three times. I was finding it hard to score and the side seemed to suffer. We had two draws with Manchester City and they were very good games. Don Revie was perfecting his deep-lying centre forward plan that would take them back to Wembley at the end of the season, this time ending as winners. In goal for them was Bert Trautmann who would play part of the time in that cup final with a broken neck. He didn't roll over and over on the floor, footballers were much harder in those days.

At the beginning of October I received a letter from the Football Association of Wales telling me I had been selected to play against England at Ninian Park, Cardiff on

22 October. After only losing 3-2 in our last meeting we were all resolved to go one better and beat England on our own soil. I was injured playing for Arsenal against Portsmouth when I came off second best in a challenge with Pompey keeper Norman Uprichard and broke three ribs. I had missed four games when the international came round but I managed to prove my fitness to the selectors and was able to take my place in the team. I was selected at outside right once more and my inside partner was Noel Kinsey of Birmingham City. Cliff Jones was back on the left wing. Once again I spent most of my match fee on buying tickets so that my family could come and watch. Glen travelled down for the game and was also able to meet her parents as she hadn't seen them since the wedding.

Pre-match preparations were basic to say the least. We were supposed to have a practice match at Coronation Park, just down the road from Ninian Park, but no one had told the groundsman and as it had been used for a Welsh League fixture that week it was in need of a good rolling. Also no one had the key to enter the ground so we all had to climb over the fence. Secondly, there was no team to play against us and when a side was hastily arranged it was one man short. And to cap it all off, the players of both sides had the same colour training kit so it was impossible to tell one side from the other.

I always enjoyed playing against Roger Byrne. I'm told that he started his career as a winger before moving to full back. Billy Wright was another that I always felt I could beat with my speed off the mark. That is how the first goal came about. Mel Charles swung the ball into the centre where Trevor Ford and Wright went up for it, missed it and it came out wide to me. As the England skipper came in to block, I pushed the ball past him and left him for dead. As I approached England keeper Bert Williams at the Canton Stand end of the ground I let fly and beat him with a shot into the corner. Cliff Jones headed in a second a minute later and we looked home and dry until Big John gave them a lifeline. A Roger Byrne cross came into the box and Charlo tried to relieve the pressure by heading the ball back to Jack Kelsey, unfortunately Jack was nowhere to be seen and it went into the corner of the net. That made it 2-1 and a very tense final few minutes but we hung on for the first win over England since a war-time international in 1945. We did it even with Roy Paul little more than a passenger for most of the second half out on the wing. Before his injury Roy had blotted out Don Revie and with Alf Sherwood sticking close to Stan Matthews, the English attack rarely got working. Towards the end of the game some of the England players resorted to a bit of the rough stuff as they couldn't handle the pace of us Welsh forwards but we stood our ground and fully deserved the victory. There was plenty of celebrating that evening I can tell you but there was no champagne in the dressing room for us. It was great to score for my country and I would go on to play England three times and score twice in a win, draw and a defeat, but that was the best of the three.

All the Wales players enjoyed the reception that evening in the Park Hotel. We didn't gloat, it was just a good feeling to have at last put one over on England. After all, I knew all the England players as I came up against them every week in the league playing for the Arsenal. Don't forget that as well as Matthews and Revie up front they also had Nat Lofthouse, Dennis Wilshaw of Wolves, and Tom Finney. Add those names to a half back line of Bill McGarry, Billy Wright and Jimmy Dickinson and you can see why we were over the moon at beating them at long last.

Poor Jeff Hall, the Birmingham full back, was given stick by the crowd for the last 15 minutes as it appeared that he had kicked me on the arm after we both went down in the England penalty area while challenging for the ball. I can tell you now that he didn't kick me intentionally, he was just trying to untangle himself and get up and on with the game. It was his international debut and I think he found it all a bit too fast for him. When the referee stopped the game for me to receive attention the crowd began booing Hall and a spectator ran on to the pitch but he was quickly removed by the stewards. It was then that the game developed into a bit of a kicking match but we held on to our lead.

It was a great shock when Jeff died of polio at the age of 30 in 1959.

My goal wasn't enough to win my place back in the Arsenal side to play Charlton Athletic the following weekend but I regained my spot the next week when we travelled to Old Trafford to face Manchester United and another meeting with Roger Byrne. Once again I failed to score and it was Doug Lishman who earned us a point in a 1-1 draw.

The international matches were now coming thick and fast and we were off to Glasgow to face Scotland on 9 November.

Two days before that however, Arsenal played Leeds United in a floodlit match at Elland Road where the stand had been burnt down just a few days previously.

It was weird changing in makeshift accommodation and walking out on to the field between the black skeletal steel remains of the stand. Jack Kelsey and I asked to be excused from the match as the Scotland game was only two days away but we were refused permission to miss the game. As it happened, it was probably the best thing that could have happened to me as we won 3-0 and I hit two of our goals past Leeds keeper Roy Wood to get back into the habit of goal-scoring. John Charles played up front for Leeds and at centre half was Jack Charlton. Jack was a difficult man to get past as he seemed to put everything in your way as you tried to get through. By fair means or foul he would do his best to keep you out and he was a good stopper. We led 2-0 at half time with Doug Lishman also scoring and I made it three near the end.

After the match Jack and I joined up with Charlo and the three of us travelled up to Glasgow together on the night sleeper to meet the rest of the Wales lads.

The game against Scotland was not much to write home about. The Scots had it sewn up by half time after two goals from Manchester City's inside right, Bobby Johnstone. Inside left that day was Bobby Collins of Celtic. He was a real tough guy who would go on to play for Everton and Leeds United. We played a little better in the second half but the 2-0 defeat was very disappointing particularly after doing so well against England.

A fortnight later we were at the Racecourse, Wrexham where Austria were the visitors. The only change in our line up was Len Allchurch coming in for Birmingham's Noel Kinsey. Len went to outside right so that meant I was in my favoured inside right spot. I scored but we lost 2-1 although it was a good performance against a very strong and physical Austrian side. But they were just about the dirtiest team I had ever played against. They thought nothing of pulling you back by the shirt, kicking you when the ball had long since gone, or digging you in the ribs. It was a French referee and he might just as well have stayed in France for all the use he was. If he had clamped down on the nonsense right from the start it wouldn't have gradually become worse. They opened up a two goal lead but then lost a player through injury after about half an hour. It looked as though he had broken his leg and he was stretchered off the field. As it was a friendly, substitutes were allowed for injuries in the first half, while goalkeepers could be changed if they were injured at any time. Soon after the sub came on the field I managed to get between their defenders and headed home to reduce the deficit.

Trevor Ford was well known for his treatment of keepers and he barged the Austrian at every opportunity. Don't forget that in those days providing the keeper was holding the ball he was fair game for a good old-fashioned shoulder charge. Between us we were giving their man, a guy called Bruno Engelmaier, a bit of a hammering and the Austrian defenders were getting more and more worked up.

Five Welsh players, including me, needed treatment after the game and Mel Charles was carried off towards the end. I had a kick in the side that injured a kidney and it genuinely took several weeks before I was completely over the effects of it. The useless referee was afraid to give us a penalty in the closing minutes when John Charles was cut down in the penalty area for a cast-iron spot-kick.

We couldn't understand the criticism that was levelled at the Welsh players as well as the Austrians after the match by even our own media. We didn't resort to the dirty tricks they did. They may not have liked us barging their keeper but that was part and parcel of the British game. Their most famous player Ernst Ocwirk was scathing in his after match comments. 'I have played in 57 international matches but this was the dirtiest I have ever played in, or even seen. The referee should have stopped the vicious attacks on our goalkeeper.'

Ocwirk was a top class player as was Hanappi, the inside forward, but they wanted time on the ball to do what they liked, they couldn't take a hard tackle.

I also had a knock on my knee but that quickly cleared up and I played three days later for the Arsenal against Burnley at Highbury.

New blood was introduced into the club when Vic Groves and Stan Charlton joined from Leyton Orient Both players understandably took some time to settle in but within a few weeks they were regular members of the starting line-up with Stan taking over at full back from Len

Wills and Vic playing usually as a number nine.

Back with Arsenal I started to find my form with eight goals in eight games helping the club move up the Division One table. I was in the wars however when we played West Brom at Highbury on 10 December. Not long after I opened the scoring I went up for the ball with their full back, Don Howe, and his elbow caught me right in the mouth, snapping my front tooth and pushing it through my lip. There was a fair bit of blood about so I went off the field to have the damage looked at. Billy Milne wiped the 'magic sponge' over my mouth and face and suggested that he pull out the remaining loose piece of tooth to prevent it waggling about, but I managed to dissuade him from carrying out such drastic action and went back out on the field to finish the match which we won 2-0.

Arsenal arranged for me to visit the dentist on the Monday after the game and while I was in the waiting room there was someone else there waiting to have a tooth removed. He introduced himself as George Gibson and said he had been an Arsenal fan for many years. He received treatment before me but when I eventually came out after my turn I found him sat down waiting for me. He suggested a cup of coffee while we chatted about Arsenal and when we had finished he took me to Covent Garden where he was one of the managers. He took hold of two bags and as we walked round the stalls he had them filled with fruit and vegetables.

George and his wife Peggy became very good friends of ours and they used to come down to stay with us along with their two children when we moved to Cardiff. The first time they came to Wales they were amazed as they expected everyone to be speaking in Welsh.

George was a grandstand season ticket holder so he never asked me to get him any tickets although I was able to provide cup tickets for him to pass on to the other lads at

Covent Garden. Every Friday if I was playing at home I would go down and get a basket filled, and when I was playing away, they would deliver one to the flat for us. When I first knew him he lived in an apartment close to Arsenal Stadium and he knew football, and the club, inside out. They were great pals of ours and helped Glen, in particular, get used to life in London.

The match after the West Brom victory contained an incident that if seen nowadays, would be shown over and over again on television. We were playing Blackpool at Highbury and everything seemed to be going right when we were leading 4-0. I had scored to add to goals from Vic Groves, Cliff Holton and Jimmy Bloomfield and we were cruising. Con Sullivan, our keeper, gathered a fairly tame shot as the game was coming to a close and he threw the ball out to Dennis Evans just as a wag in the crowd blew a whistle. Dennis thought that meant the end of the game so he blasted the ball back into the net past an astonished Con who had also heard it and was bending down picking up his gloves and cap. As for me, I was halfway down the tunnel. Needless to say, the referee didn't see the funny side of it and signalled a goal much to our disappointment as our performance that day deserved a clean sheet. Dennis never lived that own goal down and was constantly reminded of it by fans of both sides until he finished playing.

Glen went to all the matches at Highbury on her own as I had to meet the players for our pre-match meeting. All the ladies would sit in the same area and at the final whistle they would go down into the players lounge for a cup of tea. Glen usually sat by Jack Kelsey's wife Myrtle and Iris, Dennis Evans' wife. There was however one exception to the rule. Anna Neagle, the famous actress, was another celebrity who could be found at Highbury on match days. She never sat in the area provided for wives and girlfriends as she had her own seat in the directors' box.

The Christmas matches against Wolves ended all square with two draws and I beat Bert Williams twice in the 3-3 game at Highbury the day after Boxing Day. Then on the last day of 1955 we won 3-1 against Bolton Wanderers. The Wanderers had suffered three defeats over the holiday period and dropped their regular keeper Ken Grieves, who also played cricket for Lancashire, in favour of long serving Stan Hanson who had been between the sticks in the Matthews Cup Final of 1953. Poor old Stan gifted me my second goal when he failed to hold on to a Dennis Evans free kick and I tapped it in from close range. A Danny Clapton cross had given me my first just before the interval. We ended up winning quite easily but Nat Lofthouse headed a consolation goal for them. That goal by Nat came under unusual circumstances. The referee penalised Dennis Evans for a misleading call, he shouted 'Mine', and Nat nodded home directly from John Wheeler's free kick.

My brother Alan, had come up to Highbury for a trial during the season and the club wanted to take him on but for some reason he preferred life in South Wales.

The third round of the FA Cup almost turned out to be a catastrophe for the club. When we heard the draw giving us a home tie against non-league Bedford Town we all thought that was a comfortable passage into the fourth round.

As usual for big games we were taken away to a hotel to prepare. When training finished we were always given a glass of sherry into which we cracked open a raw egg. It was supposed to give us extra energy but I don't think it did anything at all. In any case, if it was that good, why didn't we have sherry and eggs all the time.

As 7 January 1956 arrived, we were all fit and ready to see off these non-leaguers. When I opened the scoring and Vic Groves added another we were coasting to the easy victory that was expected of a Division One club.

Unfortunately for us, no one had told Bedford that we were supposed to win and they kept on chasing and harrying and running for everything and deservedly struck two goals past a surprised Con Sullivan to end up with a 2-2 scoreline. This set up a replay in Bedford the following Thursday. There were no arguments amongst the players after the match and Mr Whittaker never lost his temper. All he said was 'It will be impossible for you to play as badly as that again.'

But in the replay it went from bad to worse as Bedford took the lead. They were still hanging on with just four minutes of the tie remaining. Mr Whittaker admitted afterwards that at that point he had already written it off as one of the worst defeats in Arsenal's history. But we had time for a few more attacks before the referee called a halt to the proceedings. Jimmy Bloomfield managed to get down the left and from his cross Vic Groves headed in to level the scores. The match was into injury time when Vic found himself out on the flank. The ball was worked out to him, he looped over a centre, and I dived headlong to nod the ball past the keeper for the winner from the edge of the penalty area. One newspaper report I read after the game said that I had made myself into a 'human bullet' to score the winner. We were very lucky that night as Bedford also had two goals disallowed by the referee who was Leo Callaghan of Merthyr. After the game the sporting Bedford club provided us with champagne to toast our close shave.

In round four we beat Aston Villa 4-1 and I grabbed another two to make it four cup goals for me in the first two rounds. We then beat Charlton Athletic 2-0 at the Valley at the next stage but just as we were dreaming of making it to Wembley we fell 3-1 to Birmingham City, the eventual losing finalists, at home in round six. Incidentally, it was the first match ever transmitted by Independent Television.

The directors at Arsenal had decided that Mr Whittaker,

who was not in the best of health, needed some assistance in running the club on the football side and so they brought in Alec Stock from Leyton Orient in February 1956 to work with the players under Mr Whittaker's direction. Stock introduced a number of new training techniques which did not go down very well with the senior players. The new man seemed to think that he was there to knock us into shape and that was quickly resented by everyone.

It got to the stage where the experienced players would decide on the training routines and Stock found that what he said was rarely followed or acted upon. He would stand on the touchline shouting out orders and no one would take any notice. Quite frankly he had arrived at the club with totally the wrong attitude and he was never going to win us players over. On one occasion we were practising some dead ball routines out on the field when he came across and told me to go out on the wing. I politely told him that I was an inside forward and didn't want to play out on the wing. I think he chose to pick an argument with me because I was one of the younger players. An older senior professional would have stood his ground and argued his case. When I refused to move out to the wing he told me to go straight to Mr Whittaker's office and wait for him there. A couple of the lads told me not to bother but I thought I would go to keep the peace so off I trotted to the changing rooms, showered, dressed and went up to stand outside the manager's office.

I had no intention of knocking on the door and going in but Miss Grosvenor had seen me standing there and she went and found Mr Whittaker who was not in his office at the time. He came straight down and took me into his office to find out what it was all about. He told me to sit down and then I related everything that had happened that day and in the few days before. When I finished he went behind his desk and sat down with a worried look on his brow.

There is a story going about that he then poured out a couple of glasses of dry sherry for us to enjoy but I don't know where that came from although I suspect Tommy Lawton had something to do with that version going around the circuit. We continued our talk about the club and Mr Whittaker told me that he would sort out the problems as he didn't want the players to be unhappy. At that point there was a knock on the door and Stock came in. He was not best pleased when he saw me happily chatting away with Mr Whittaker and I thought I would be better off out of it so I quickly made an exit.

I don't know what happened then, or whether me being found in the office with the manager had any bearing on later events. We played at Sheffield United on the Saturday and Stock was told not to travel with the team. While in Sheffield, the senior players had a meeting with Mr Whittaker and the younger players, me included along with the two lads from Stock's former club Leyton Orient, Vic Groves and Stan Charlton, were not allowed to attend. Things were brought to a head and Stock was forced to resign as his position was quite clearly untenable and he returned to his previous post at Leyton Orient. I don't know whether that can be classed as player power or not. I prefer to say that an individual came to the club who was not an Arsenal man and his methods were not Arsenal methods, so when he realised that fact he resigned and went back to his previous employment.

On the league front we finished the season with seven wins from our last eight matches and I scored in each of the last three games, including a 2-1 win at Ninian Park against Cardiff City in the final game of the season. They had a good young centre forward playing for them that day called Gerry Hitchens and he scored their goal. It was the first time I had met Brian Walsh since he left Highbury for Cardiff and we had a good chat over old times at the end of

The Tapscott family outside our house in Queen Street in 1945. The only one missing is Geoff who didn't arrive until 1947.

I am holding the South Wales Senior Cup after Barry Town defeated Cardiff City 3-0 in the 1953 final.

10 April 1954. A great moment as I score my first goal in league football with Liverpool keeper Dave Underwood beaten. Arsenal 3 Liverpool 0.

Boarding the plane for Austria with Stewart Williams just behind me. For once we are in front of members of the First Team.

*9 May 1954.
Giving the
Austrian keeper a
bit of stick in
Vienna.
Note the square-
section wooden
goalposts. Austria
2 Wales 0.*

*4 September 1954. Spurs keeper Ted Ditchburn makes a flying save at Highbury with
Alf Ramsey in support behind him. Arsenal 2 Spurs 0*

11 September 1954. I score Arsenal's third goal at Highbury in our 4-0 victory over Sheffield Utd. The Blades keeper is Alan Hodgkinson.

27 November 1954. On the attack against Wolves but Bert Williams saves. On the left is Billy Wright. Arsenal 1 Wolves 1.

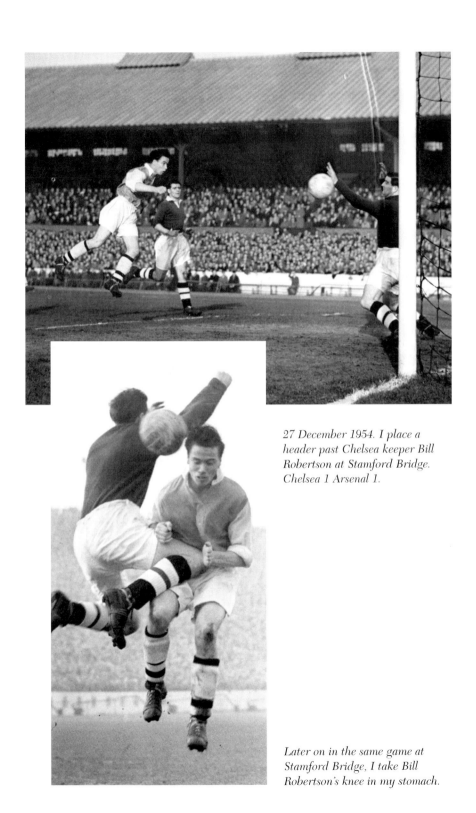

27 December 1954. I place a header past Chelsea keeper Bill Robertson at Stamford Bridge. Chelsea 1 Arsenal 1.

Later on in the same game at Stamford Bridge, I take Bill Robertson's knee in my stomach.

Our Wedding day. 9 July, 1955 at St Mary's Church, Barry Dock.

15 October 1955. Ronnie Simpson of Newcastle clears the ball during our 1-0 victory at Highbury. In the background is Mike Tiddy.

Arsenal's four Wales internationals in training. Left to right; Jack Kelsey, Walley Barnes, me and Dave Bowen.

31 December 1955. I take the ball around Bolton keeper Stan Hanson to score Arsenal's third goal in a 3-1 victory over Bolton. In the background is Vic Groves.

7 January 1956. I score the first goal in the problematic FA Cup tie against Bedford Town at Highbury. Arsenal 2 Bedford Town 2.

26 January 1957. On this occasion, I shoot wide in the FA Cup tie at Somerton Park against Newport County but we still come away with a 2-0 win. The Newport keeper is Len Weare and on the right is Alf Sherwood.

Leaving the Royal Northern Hospital after my cartilage operation in 1957.

26 November 1958. I find the net for Wales against England at Villa Park. The goalkeeper is Colin McDonald. England 2 Wales 2.

The Busby Babes final league game on 1 February 1958. Tommy Taylor (9) scores United's third goal watched by Dennis Viollet (10). I am doing some defending (8), along with Dennis Evans (3) and Jim Fotheringham (5). Arsenal 4 Manchester Utd 5.

23 January 1959. At Cardiff General Station starting a trip to Norwich for an FA Cup 4th round tie.

The 1959-60 promotion-winning squad. Left to right (back row); Joe Bonson, Alec Milne, Ron Nicholls, Graham Vearncombe, Colin Baker, Derrick Sullivan, Ron Stitfall, (middle row); Brian Walsh, me, Danny Malloy, Graham Moore, Johnny Watkins, (front row); Harry Knowles, Alan Harrington, Steve Mokone, Alan Durban, Colin Hudson.

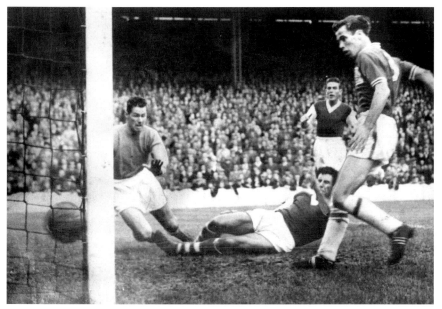

24 October 1959. A poacher's goal. Ipswich keeper Roy Bailey is beaten and I'm left with a tap-in as Cardiff City beat Ipswich Town 3-2.

21 November 1959. A typical diving header of mine makes it 1-1 at Ninian Park against Stoke City. Cardiff City 4 Stoke City 4.

7 April 1960. Graham Moore scores the only goal in a game against Aston Villa that takes Cardiff City back to Division One.

4 November 1961. I score the winner at Craven Cottage against Fulham with a far post header. Also in the picture left to right; Eddie Lowe (Fulham), Tony Pickrell (Cardiff), George Cohen (Fulham) and Tony Macedo (Fulham). Fulham 0 Cardif City 1.

Cardiff manager George Swindin with coach Ernie Curtis in the centre and newly-appointed trainer Stan Montgomery. December 1962.

*The first draw for Cardiff City's BIF and BAF. Left to right; George Swindin
(manager), George Edwards (director), Fred Dewey (director), Graham Keenor
(secretary), me and Colin Baker.*

*August 1964. New manager Jimmy Scoular leads the City players in training at
Coronation Park. I am just behind the boss.*

The Cardiff City players get ready to embark for the trip to play Real Zaragoza in the Cup Winners Cup in January 1965.

My Grandsons, Jaimie and Gareth from Cheltenham, and Haydn who lives in Bahrain.

the match. Strangely enough, neither Mike Tiddy nor Gordon Nutt were in the Arsenal line-up that day proving once again that Cardiff definitely had the better of that strange transfer deal. At centre half for City was a big brawny Scot named Danny Malloy who I got to know quite well when I later joined the Bluebirds. Danny was hard, so much so that he would probably have kicked his own grandmother if it meant stopping the opposition scoring. He was a player who never took any prisoners.

I finished the season as Arsenal's top scorer with 17 league goals from 31 appearances. Vic Groves and Cliff Holton were next with eight goals as the club improved dramatically to finish in fifth place in Division One.

At the end of the season, 4 May, I was delighted to be selected in a London XI to play City of Basle in the Inter-Cities Fairs Cup at White Hart Lane. The team was picked from clubs all over London by Joe Mears, the Chelsea chairman, and Jack Kelsey was chosen to play in goals. The Inter-Cities Fairs Cup, later to become the UEFA Cup, was started in 1955, the same time as the European Champions Cup. As no English or Welsh club had entered the Champions Cup at that time, Jack and I were the first Welshmen to play in a recognised European competition and we were both very proud of that honour. We won the match 1-0 with a very late goal from Spurs winger George Robb. Danny Blanchflower, also of Spurs, was the skipper and I was at inside right with my Arsenal team-mate Cliff Holton at number nine.

Organisation was not like it is nowadays and that first cup competition did not reach a conclusion until May 1958, three years after it started, when the London XI were beaten 6-0 at the Nou Camp by Barcelona in the second leg after the first game at Stamford Bridge was drawn 2-2. Jack played in both legs of the final but by then I had cartilage problems so could not be considered.

We finished up the season with our usual tour to Switzerland and Germany which was a good way of winding down after the season's exertions.

9

GOAL JOY AND HEARTACHE

During the summer months, Glen and I were able to visit my sister Violet in Willesden and also my other sister Vera who lived in Oxford. We also started playing tennis on a nearby court and that was very relaxing. Most of the lads enjoyed a game of cricket and Arsenal had a team that used to play every now and again for charity. While I was with the club we often played at Tufnell Park or perhaps Horsmonden. I remember once playing against a Denis Compton XI when it seemed that most of the Middlesex side were in the opposition as well as Godfrey Evans, the famous Kent wicketkeeper. But we could call on Leslie Compton and Don Bennett who also played for Middlesex, and of course Arthur Milton who played for Gloucestershire and was the last player to be capped by England at both cricket and football, so we could put out a more than useful side. Tommy Lawton was a better than average batsman when he was at the club and Don Roper could bat and bowl to a good standard.

In the summer evenings Glen and I would go to the cinema or perhaps the Finsbury Park Empire to see a show. Any time you wanted tickets for anything you only had to let the Arsenal office know and they would arrange to have them sent to the club.

Many of the top stars of the day were Arsenal supporters such as Bill Maynard, Greengrass from TV's Heartbeat, Dave King, the singer and comedian, Pete Murray the radio disc jockey and presenter of Six-Five Special, Ralph Reader the showman, and singer Tony Dalli, and we became friendly with all of them over a period of time. Stan Stennett was another star we got to know socially through the Arsenal connection. In fact, many years later when we had been invited back to the club for a big match, we were standing on the platform of a tube station when I heard someone shout out 'Tappy'. I looked around and there was Pete Murray who we hadn't seen for several years. It was good to see him once again and I thought it remarkable that he remembered me after such a long time.

In July, I managed to get hold of tickets for a show in Cardiff and Glen was delighted with the opportunity of going back home as it gave us a rare chance to see our families. She was a little less pleased when she found out that the tickets were for a boxing show at Maindy Stadium with Dick Richardson, the London milkman, and Dai Dower on the bill.

The only theatre performances I couldn't stand were opera and ballet, but I was handed a lifeline here by none other than my team-mate Bill Dodgin. He was really keen on opera so we came to an arrangement where he took Glen to the opera and any ballet that was on in the West End while I was able to stay at home. I was quite happy for Glen to go and knew she would be safe in Bill's company.

A few times we would make up a foursome with Jack Kelsey and his wife Myrtle, usually going to see the latest film at the cinema. We also went on holiday with them one year to Ostend.

It was through Jack and Myrtle that we first met Bob Silva and his wife Sylvia. We started meeting up during the summer and would go off for little picnics. Bob had a big car and he used to drive around picking everyone up. He was in the clothing trade and a real Arsenal fanatic who would never ever miss a game and he loved being in the company of us Arsenal lads. When we eventually moved into our first house, he arranged all the furniture at a good price. We kept in touch for many years even after I retired from football. They were lovely people.

Across the road from our flat was a big church set in its own grounds. We started going there regularly until I had to report to Highbury on Sunday mornings for extra training or perhaps some medical attention, so Glen usually went on her own.

We were becoming very friendly with Dave King who was a keen Arsenal fan. Whenever he was in London for a show he would ring us up and make sure we had tickets. After the performances we would all go out to a restaurant. Dave wanted a house in our area so for a few evenings every week we took him on a tour of the neighbourhood, but he never found anything that he liked.

Every year Arsenal would play Racing Club of Paris in a challenge match. The first meeting was back in 1930 so it was a well-established event. We used to play them alternately home and away. My first match against them was at Highbury when we won 4-0. I managed to stoop low to head into the net for the opening goal and we scored the others after the interval. The big talking point in the game however was the old chestnut of shoulder-charging foreign keepers. Every time their man caught hold of the ball he would take ages in getting rid of it, so Cliff Holton and me would use a bit of persuasion to make him move a little faster. Every time we approached the keeper a ring of French defenders would move menacingly in on us but luckily it was a British referee and he made sure they stayed well away.

I enjoyed spending a few days in Paris and one of the matches in France really stands out. It was in October 1956 and was the 20th meeting between the two sides. Racing were at that time one of the top clubs in France and they had five full internationals in their team as well as a number of Under-23 caps.

In the Arsenal tradition, the full party left in two planes from Heathrow and there was a scare as the first plane to leave had to turn back because of a fault. We stayed at Claridges Hotel on the Champs Elysees and had an early night after our arrival. A light training session at the Colombes Stadium the next morning was followed by a sightseeing trip to the Palace of Versailles before a lengthy wait for the evening kick-off. When the match eventually kicked off, everything went right for us in that first half. Cliff Holton put me through early on and I opened the scoring. A few minutes later Danny Clapton flicked the ball to me and I scored again. Midway through the opening period I made it a hat-trick when the Racing defence failed to clear and I nipped in to net from close range.

Anglo-French relations took a turn for the worse when I shoulder-charged the keeper who promptly punched me in the face, but the referee chose to completely ignore it. Early in the second half I scored a perfectly good goal when I outpaced their defenders but the referee wrongly disallowed it for offside, perhaps he was paying me back for all those hits on their keeper. They gradually piled on the pressure and pulled a couple of goals back but then little Joe Haverty whipped over a cross and I knocked it in to make it a very memorable evening from my point of view. Racing pulled another one back but we held out for a very good 4-3 win and I was very satisfied with my first four-goal haul in an Arsenal shirt.

The new 1956-57 season opened with Cardiff City once again the first visitors to Highbury. They had also started our home season off the previous year as well as being the last club we played to finish off the season. I was at inside right and Mike Tiddy played on the left wing for us. Charlie Rutter, who still has a pet shop upstairs in Cardiff Central Market, was at right back for the Bluebirds, my old pal Brian Walsh was on the wing, and up front for the City were Trevor

Ford and Gerry Hitchens. It was a funny old game with both sides having chances to pinch a win but it ended better for Cardiff who went home well pleased with a point after a 0-0 draw.

I had to wait until September before scoring my first league goal of what would turn out to be my best season in Arsenal colours. We had suffered two defeats at Birmingham and Burnley but when West Brom came to Highbury we found our true form and won convincingly 4-1. Don Roper scored the first two, I had the third and then Mike Tiddy rounded it off.

We were very inconsistent in the early part of the season and a win would be followed by a defeat until the FA Cup holders Manchester City came to Highbury. All of a sudden we could do no wrong and Cliff Holton banged in four as we won 7-3. Strangely enough I never scored in that match but I bagged a double the following week when we beat Charlton Athletic 3-1. That was the week the Wales side to play Scotland in Cardiff was announced and I was shattered to find that after playing in nine consecutive international matches I had been left out of the line-up. Terry Medwin of Spurs was picked at outside right and filling my number eight shirt was Big John himself. On the day Scotland drew 2-2 with Wales, Fordy and Medwin scoring our goals, I was at Highbury playing for Arsenal against a Spurs side missing Medwin of course and full back Mel Hopkins. I didn't get on the scoresheet but I helped David Herd notch a couple in a 3-1 win over our fiercest rivals.

Four days later, 24 October, 1956, we were given the sad news that the manager, Mr Whittaker, had died in University College Hospital where he had undergone an operation a few months earlier. It was a terrible blow as you wouldn't find a more honest and genuine man. He would find the time to listen to any problems whether it was football or personal, and he would always do his best to help you. There would never be any public roasting after a poor display, and a pat on the back from him was like winning the cup. I will never forget that knowing wink when he caught sight of my birth certificate and promised never to reveal its secret.

All the playing staff chipped in to buy a wreath which simply said 'To Tom from all the Boys' and it took pride of place on top of the hearse for everyone to see. We all attended the funeral service which was held at St James's Church. All the big names in football were there to pay their respects to a great man.

By a strange coincidence, that was the week that we left our flat in Turnpike Lane and moved in to our first club house which was in Brunswick Park Road, New Southgate. The club had told us that as soon as a club property became available we would be given the first chance of having it. We fell in love with the house the moment we first set eyes on it. It had stained glass windows in the front and the hall, high ceilings, and big well laid-out gardens. It was a beautiful place with superb views and Glen and I were thrilled at the prospect of living there. The Arsenal lads were surprised that we had agreed to move there as they reckoned it was a jinx house. Reg Lewis, the old centre forward, moved in, had a succession of injuries, and lost his place in the team. Bill Dickson, the same Bill who signed for the club the very day I did, also suffered a whole load of injury problems that would eventually bring his career to a premature end. He had left the club just before the start of the season to join Mansfield in an effort to try and resurrect his career and the house had been vacant since then. But we scoffed at all the talk as we were not superstitious. That would turn out to be a big mistake.

Mr Whittaker's death put the loss of my Wales place into perspective but strangely enough, the chances started coming my way not long after that and I scored seven goals in a five-game spell. It still wasn't enough to convince the selectors to bring me back for a trip to Wembley to meet England, though the only change when the side was announced was up front where Trevor Ford was replaced by Mel Charles who was playing for Swansea Town at that time. Brother John scored but Wales were beaten 3-1.

Not having to play an international match midweek seemed to agree with me as when Bolton Wanderers came to Highbury the following Saturday, I scored my second brace in successive games. We beat Bolton Wanderers 3-0 quite easily, Cliff Holton banged in the other, to set up a run of ten games without defeat that shot us up the table.

The Christmas Day and Boxing Day fixtures were kind to us as we didn't have to travel very far. We played Chelsea at Stamford Bridge first and drew 1-1 before winning the Boxing Day match 2-0 with Danny Clapton scoring the first before I settled it towards the end of the game. Peter Sillett was a real hard man at full back for Chelsea and we went hammer and tongs during both games. Afterwards, in the players room at Highbury, we enjoyed a chat over a cup of tea and a smoke because once the match was over we were all friends and there was a mutual respect.

Because of the matches over the holiday period, it was a quiet Christmas for us in the house in new Southgate. Glen bought me a complete set of golf clubs as I was becoming hooked on the game. I still have them to this day but styles have changed now and it is some time since I was able to use them.

We still met up with our friends whenever possible but it is difficult when you have to watch what you are eating, and drinking while still in strict training and there was no chance of getting home to South Wales. That was the very last time fixtures were arranged for Christmas Day and I think that was a good thing. In any case, it was becoming far more difficult to travel over the Christmas period and even if the clubs could make the necessary arrangements for the players, the supporters were often hard-pressed to follow their teams up and down the country.

Jack Crayston became manager in the December, and that was a choice happily accepted by all the players. It had been Jack who had welcomed me when I made my Arsenal debut at Queens Park Rangers in the London Combination when I first arrived at Highbury in what seemed a long time ago.

Mr Crayston, as he had now become of course, had the FA Cup to think about almost immediately and in January 1957 we played Stoke City at home in the third round. I scored one in a 4-2 win which set up an intriguing fourth round match away to giantkillers Newport County. Playing at small grounds like Somerton Park could sometimes land you in trouble and with a lot of my family able to travel the 20 miles or so from Barry to watch the game, I was determined that Arsenal would not suffer a shock defeat.

There was an old friend of mine in the County line-up as Alf Sherwood had joined them at the start of the season from Cardiff City. There was even more Cardiff interest as former Bluebird Ken Hollyman failed a late fitness test and Arthur 'Buller' Lever, yet another ex-City player, took over at right back. It had been wet all week but a strong wind on the day of the game helped dry the pitch out.

It didn't take long for us to go into the lead. With just five minutes on the clock I found myself in possession inside the penalty area and I had time to pick my spot and blast the ball past Len Weare in the Newport goal. Len made a number of fine saves and I thought I had doubled the lead but he somehow turned my shot round the corner. He was a good keeper for County for many seasons and would surely have won caps for Wales if he had been playing regularly at a higher level. But it wasn't all Arsenal. Before half time big Pat Terry had a good chance but Con Sullivan managed to keep his shot out.

We decided on a shoot on sight policy for the second half and but for Len in the home goal we would have been home and dry well before the end of play. As it was, it took us until the final minute when a Jimmy Bloomfield shot rebounded to David Herd and he banged it home to seal the win. It was an excellent display by the Third Division side in front of a packed Somerton Park with close on 22,500 spectators jammed in. They battled away throughout the 90 minutes.

Once the Newport tie was out of the way we continued with the league programme by beating Sheffield Wednesday 6-3. I scored twice but the star of the show was our new up and coming centre forward, David Herd who claimed a hat-trick. David had been signed from Stockport a couple of years previously and football was definitely in his blood. His father Alec had played for Scotland and David actually made his league debut for Stockport lining up alongside his dad when he was just 17 years old. Mr Whittaker had signed him as soon as he had finished his national service and he also went on to play for Scotland. He proved to be a very good player for Arsenal, averaging a goal every other game, and in that year's cup matches he scored in all but one of our six games.

Preston were next up in round five and we did well to draw 3-3 at Deepdale where Tom Finney was in fine form. Sometimes it was difficult to decide whether Finney or Stan Matthews were the better proposition at outside right. Tom scored more goals but Stan had more tricks up his sleeve. Perhaps the best solution was to play Tom at centre forward with Stan out on the wing.

The return at Highbury three days later was a really tough game but a very rare goal from my good pal Bill Dodgin helped us scrape through 2-1. West Brom and the Hawthorns now lay between us and a quarter-final place. Once again, with players like Ronnie Allen up front, Ray Barlow at wing half, and Frank Griffin on the wing they were a good side who could always be counted upon to get stuck in. We were delighted to come away with a 2-2 draw but should have realised how lucky we were when it was Stan Charlton, our full back, who scored to bring them back to Highbury.

Sure enough, three days after holding them in the Midlands, they knocked us out 2-1 with wing half Cliff Holton scoring for us. It was very disappointing after seemingly doing all the hard work away and getting so near to the last eight.

Our cup form was poor but my golf was improving by leaps and bounds. Once a week, usually on a Wednesday if there was no midweek match, a few of us would go off for a round or two. I really enjoyed it and in time became quite useful. I never got down to scratch but I did eventually get my handicap into single figures.

We lost 3-1 at home to Luton in the league in our next match, a sort of anti-climax, but then picked up and only lost twice in the last nine or ten games to the end of the season. We finished fifth, six points behind champions Manchester United, the same position as the previous season. I was delighted with my form and didn't want the season to end. I scored five times in the Easter matches against Blackpool, home and away, and Charlton Athletic, to finish the season for the second successive time as the club top scorer with 25 goals from 38 games.

To add to my delight, I was recalled to the Wales side to play Northern Ireland in Belfast on 10 April after Ivor Allchurch had withdrawn through injury. I would rather have been named as first choice but at least I was back in the side and determined to stay there. The big surprise was that Alf Sherwood had been dropped. Trevor Edwards of Charlton Athletic made his debut at right back and there was also a first cap for Roy Vernon of Blackburn Rovers. Both players were still doing their national service. Believe it or not,

Trevor was a steward and Roy worked as a pay clerk, so not much soldiering training needed there then. By a strange coincidence, it was also the first time a Wales side had not included a single player from Cardiff City for over ten years.

Ray Daniel of Sunderland was late reporting in as he was forced to play for his club against Aston Villa on the Monday, two days before the international. When he finally arrived he was struggling with a leg injury and it was touch and go as to whether he would be fit to play. Wales physio Bill Bodman worked on him throughout Tuesday and the morning of the match and he made it to the starting line-up.

With wingers like Terry Medwin and Cliff Jones and a centre forward called John Charles you would have thought that was a recipe for goals, goals and more goals, but it just didn't work out like that. It was a completely forgettable game that ended 0-0 mainly because the Irish refused to go forward and kept everyone behind the ball. I went close a couple of times but the hard going and windy conditions made it difficult. I had one shot that looked a goal all the way until Bertie Peacock deflected it for a corner. It was just our luck when Charlo hit the post with a header in the final minute with Irish keeper Harry Gregg well beaten.

Everyone wanted to put on a good performance to catch the selectors eyes as there were two World Cup qualifiers coming up in May. The 1958 World Cup Finals were being held in Sweden and we felt that we had the players in the squad that could get us to the finals of a big competition for the first time.

Six days after the Northern Ireland game in Belfast the selectors announced a squad of 20 players for the forthcoming matches. They were Czechoslovakia in Cardiff, East Germany in Leipzig, and then the return against Czechoslovakia in Prague, all three being part of the World Cup qualification. I was delighted to be named along with team-mates Jack Kelsey and Dave Bowen while Cardiff City also had a representative as Ron Stitfall was included in the list of defenders.

Once again though, when the team was announced, I was left out in favour of Roy Vernon. I couldn't understand the selectors way of thinking. I was the top goal scorer for a club that finished in fifth place in Division One, while Roy, who played in Division Two with Blackburn had scored very few goals in the season just ended. Another shock was the inclusion of Manchester United's Colin Webster who was selected at centre forward even though he had played mainly out on the wing for his club.

The big news of the day that overshadowed everything else was Big John leaving Leeds United and signing for Juventus. Although it was a great move for John, there was also the doubt as to whether the Italians would let him play for Wales. In the event they did and he lined up at centre half as Ray Daniel was suspended sine die by the Football League after he and five other players refused to talk at an enquiry into illegal payments at Sunderland. My luck changed a little when Ivor Allchurch once again failed to recover from his leg injury and I was brought into the team at inside right with Roy switching to Ivor's inside left position.

We trained at Ninian Park but we were handicapped because of the absence of three members of the team. Charlo was now in Italy, while Terry Medwin and Mel Hopkins were made to play for Spurs against Burnley on the Monday before the international. I couldn't understand the logic in Tottenham making them both play as Spurs were already assured of finishing in second place in the league. That was the sort of thing Wales had to put up with in those days and it was something that happened to me several times during my career.

The match against the Czechs was unique as it was the first time Wales had played in a World Cup qualifier as previously the Home Championships had been used as an eliminator.

Fortunately, Big John was released in time to play and he did very well for us. He was mobbed at the final whistle as the crowd ran on to the field. Jack Kelsey also had one of his best games for Wales. We won 1-0 with the goal coming near the end. Cliff Jones slipped a pass inside to me and I crossed to the far post where Terry Medwin nodded it down and Roy Vernon smashed it home.

It was a great feeling to start our World Cup campaign with a win and now our thoughts were all on the next game in East Germany.

The side to play in Leipzig was announced three days after the victory over the Czechs and I was very relieved when I found myself named in the starting line-up.

It wasn't feet up for me though as I immediately left to join the Arsenal lads for the end of season tour which took us to Sweden where we were due to play three or four games. I had a knock on the knee in the opening match in Stockholm. Billy Milne applied the magic sponge and I finished the game though in some discomfort. In the evening the knee became quite swollen and I was forced to miss the remaining matches. That injury would come back to haunt me but it had cleared up by the time I joined the rest of the Wales squad when we reported to our hotel in Weybridge, Surrey prior to departing for East Germany.

We flew in to Leipzig Airport and stayed at a comfortable hotel not far from the stadium. The match itself proved to be a nightmare because Dave Bowen broke a couple of ribs and I chipped my ankle bone. A Mel Charles goal couldn't save us from a 2-1 defeat and on we went to Prague to meet Czechoslovakia.

The selectors were now presented with big problems as Dave was unfit to play and I was certainly out of the reckoning. A call was put out to Ray Daniel whose suspension had been lifted, and he came in to play centre half with Big John moving up front where he was partnered by Swansea's Des Palmer.

I sat in the dugout to watch the game next to Jimmy Murphy and in all honesty, we never got going against a typically strong Czech side who won 2-0. As long as you gave Jimmy Murphy 100% he would do right by you. Mind you, his language could only be described as colourful, but there is little harm in that and he was a very genuine person, it was just that on that day we were definitely second best.

Ray Daniel played in a new pair of boots and he suffered for it because at half time he came off the field, took off his boots and his feet were covered in blood where his blisters had burst. How he finished the match I will never know but he should have known better. Every player worth his salt understands that you have to gradually wear in new boots over a period of time.

After that short trip to Eastern Europe I had a month to rest up and relax as I was determined to win my place back in the starting line-up for the new season.

Before that however, Mr Hill-Wood, the Arsenal chairman, asked me to open a garden fete at his home in Basingstoke. It was in aid of a charity and there was a big marquee set up in the grounds of his large house. Glen and I spent a few hours there but were then taken by car to the railway station where we caught a train to London as we had been given tickets for the final night of the 'Dave King Show' at the London Palladium. Dave had sent them to the club for us with a note to say that we had to be there. Little did I know that I would be making my one and only stage appearance at the Palladium. Glen and I spent the whole of the show backstage until Howard Jones, a fine singer from Wales, and Dave decided that I should wear a dinner jacket and bow tie. Howard found the clothes that fitted me and then Dave sent someone to his car to collect a pair of shoes as he felt the ones I was wearing didn't do the new outfit justice. I changed in Dave's dressing room and when I was ready they had me standing in the wings. Dave introduced me as a new up-and-coming singer and I walked out in front of a packed house. Now I can assure you that I might be Welsh, but a singer I am certainly not and there was no way I was going to sing in public that evening. Thankfully Dave told everyone who I really was and I then made my escape to the side of the stage. That evening we all enjoyed a lovely meal at a restaurant nearby. It was a great night.

10

A CARTILAGE AND A PLANE CRASH

The ankle recovered in time for me to play a couple of games of cricket with the lads. When pre-season training commenced I had forgotten all about it and for the first week or so everything was fine. Then, in a friendly little kick-about, I went for a ball with Bill Dodgin and we both kicked it at the same time. The pain shot up my right leg and seemed to stop at my knee which had become locked, the classic condition for cartilage problems. I was assisted back to the dressing room where Billy Milne had a quick look at it but I think he feared the worst as he suggested we call the club doctor in for a closer and more detailed inspection.

I had to hobble home and return two days later on the Wednesday to see the club physician. He took one look at my knee, confirmed it was indeed cartilage trouble, and said that he would arrange for a Harley Street specialist to have a look. By Friday afternoon I was in the Royal Northern Hospital being operated on. When they took the damaged cartilage out they also found a cyst and two blood clots which were all cleared up at the same time. I had 14 stitches in two cuts and resigned myself to two weeks stuck in a hospital bed.

After finishing the previous season once again as the club's top scorer I wanted to prove to myself that I could go on scoring goals at the highest level but this injury was a severe setback. Normally, cartilage operations meant being away from football for anything up to about ten weeks, and sometimes even longer so it was no way to prepare for a new season. Billy Milne started coming in to see me two days after the operation. Straightaway he had me doing leg exercises to avoid muscle waste and every day until I was allowed to return home, he came in each afternoon and we worked away at retaining at least some of my fitness.

But of course the 1957-58 season did start without me. Danny Clapton played at outside right and David Herd was inside him. The lads did very well and were unbeaten after the first four games, three of which were won.

I went back to Highbury using a walking stick but as soon as Billy saw me hobbling along the corridor he took it off me, broke it in two, and said I didn't need a stick. From that moment on he helped me with more exercises on my leg and my recovery was painful, but quick. Up in the gymnasium at Highbury he rigged up a machine with ropes and pulleys and used it to strengthen my leg muscles.

It was not until the 12th game of the season, the derby at White Hart Lane against Spurs, that I finally won a place back in the first team. I had been proving my fitness in the reserves and thought my recall was long overdue even though we were well up the table after seven wins and a draw from those opening matches. It didn't go well against Spurs for me or the side and we were beaten 3-1 with Cliff Holton scoring our goal from the wing half position. My Wales team-mate Mel Hopkins could dish it out when he wanted to and with Arsenal against Spurs derby games having an extra edge to them, coming up against Mel always left you knowing you had been in a game. It was strange really because with White Hart Lane being so close to Highbury we used to meet a lot of the Spurs players when we went out shopping with our wives.

I was dropped in favour of Gordon Nutt for the next match, which really was adding insult to injury, but he only lasted a couple of games in my place before I came back for the short trip to Stamford Bridge and a meeting with Chelsea. That finished 0-0 but I managed to put my name on the scoresheet when Manchester City came to Highbury the following week and we won 2-1 with Jimmy Bloomfield also on target.

Just as I thought things were getting a little better, Nottingham Forest slammed us 4-0 at their ground and Mr Crayston brought Vic Groves back into the side and I was dropped to the reserves.

In December, 1957, Ron Greenwood was appointed coach as the club tried hard to improve on the poor start to the season by introducing new ideas. Greenwood had retired from playing with Fulham the previous season and had starting out on a managerial career with non-league Eastbourne United. He had a number of new coaching ideas that stimulated the players for a short time. One of his experiments involved equipping players with radio transmitters so that they could receive instructions during training. If you were a ball player like Jimmy Bloomfield or Danny Clapton then you were in the Greenwood clique. Players like me who used enthusiasm and effort, though we weren't lacking completely in skill, found themselves way down his list of priorities and well outside his circle. Some of the players enjoyed his variation of training and I know that David Herd found it very stimulating to be trying out new exercise regimes almost every week. But it didn't last long as the results were no better and Greenwood left to continue a coaching career elsewhere that would eventually lead to him briefly taking the England manager's job.

When the FA Cup came around once again Arsenal were drawn against Northampton Town who were then in Division Three. Although I stayed at home to play for the reserves, Dennis Evans told me what happened on the coach taking the players to the County Ground. He said he told Mr Crayston he no longer wanted to skipper the side and the captaincy was immediately handed to my Welsh international colleague Dave Bowen. Dave kept the armband until he was transferred 18 months later to Northampton Town. It had little effect however as in one of the biggest cup shocks of all time, little Northampton knocked Arsenal out of the cup 3-1, winning quite comfortably.

Mr Crayston was forced to make changes after that horror show and I was brought back to face Blackpool at Highbury. Still in the side was Gordon Nutt who had been playing regularly at outside left instead of Joe Haverty. David Herd bagged two goals but it wasn't enough as Stan Matthews and Stan Mortensen worked their magic together and they won 3-2. My confidence was not all that good and I fully expected to be left out of the team to travel to Leicester but the only changes were in defence where Stan Charlton replaced Len Wills and Jim Fotheringham played at centre half for Bill Dodgin. This time there was a happy ending as Vic Groves scored the only goal of the game to give us our first win in five attempts.

We had a blank Saturday so Glen and I went home to Barry for a short weekend to see our families. As soon as we left her parents house to travel back to London she told me that she was worried about her father's health as he had seemed very quiet and had not even come to the door to say goodbye. No sooner had we arrived back home when we received a call to say he had died suddenly not long after we had left. It was a great shock as only a few hours previously we had all been together.

The club gave me permission to attend the funeral which was arranged for 31 January, 1958, the day before the visit of Manchester United, providing of course I was back in plenty of time to prepare for the game.

I travelled back to Barry and attended the funeral

service and after the ceremony was complete, I was forced to leave Glen with her mother and catch the early train back to London.

This was one game I definitely wanted to play in as I was looking forward to renewing acquaintances with Roger Byrne. It would turn out to be one of the most poignant matches ever played as five days later, five of United's players were killed in the Munich air crash, including my old friend and adversary Byrne.

The United team at Highbury would be the same eleven that would do duty in that second leg of that European Cup tie in Belgrade. Harry Gregg was in goal and the full backs were Bill Foulkes and Byrne. The half back line was Eddie Colman, Mark Jones and Duncan Edwards and up front were Ken Morgans, Bobby Charlton, Tommy Taylor, Denis Viollet and Albert Scanlon.

As far as the match was concerned, by the end of the first half our defence had been cracked three times. The great Duncan Edwards had powered a shot past Jack Kelsey early on, then the young Bobby Charlton hit an equally unstoppable drive to put them well on top. Edwards was a giant of a man streets ahead of anyone else in his favoured half back position. Before the half time whistle, Tommy Taylor finished off a move started by Kenny Morgans and we trooped off the field for a cup of tea looking down and out. It stayed that way until halfway into the second half when in an astonishing turnaround, we scored three goals in a fantastic three minute spell.

David Herd hit a spectacular shot that may have been one of the reasons he would later go north and join United, Vic Groves leapt high to head in a cross from Nutt, and straight from the kick-off another Nutt centre was met by a diving header from Jimmy Bloomfield. The crowd went wild, but United kept their composure to show just what a great side they were. Back they came to retake the lead through Dennis Viollet, and when Taylor knocked in their fifth from an acute angle it looked lost once again for the Arsenal. With time running out, I managed to race clear between Eddie Colman and Mark Jones and as Harry Gregg came out to narrow the angle I slotted it home for the ninth and final goal of a pulsating game that would have been remembered for the football even without the subsequent sorrow of so many dying in the tragedy the following week. There were over 60,000 spectators in Highbury that day and I guarantee you that not one person left the ground before the referee blew for time.

On a personal basis, that goal was also the last one I scored while playing for the Arsenal first team.

I was in the players lounge after the game when someone put their hand on my shoulder. I looked around and it was Roger Byrne. 'That was some game, Tappy,' he said. 'I wouldn't want to be playing games like that every week.' I told him it was even worse when you end up on the losing side in front of your own fans but he just laughed and went over to get a cup of tea. I always got on well with all the United lads, that is why the whole episode was so hard to take.

They only stayed in the lounge out of courtesy for a few brief minutes as they had to get away from London fairly quickly because of preparing for the trip to Belgrade and the match against Red Star the following Wednesday. I would have liked to have had a few words with Matt Busby to wish him well in Belgrade but managers rarely came into the players lounge and the next time I saw him it was on television as he was in a hospital bed fighting for his life.

Less than a week later the Manchester United club was torn apart in that plane crash in Munich and everyone in football lost a friend on that snow-swept runway.

It was difficult for anyone to take their minds off the tragedy but football had to go on and the United lads who perished would have wanted that. I'm sure I am not the only player from that era who remembers that it was Roger Byrne, Eddie Colman, Mark Jones, Duncan Edwards and Tommy Taylor from that great team who lost their lives that day.

I kept my place in a 2-1 home defeat by Bolton Wanderers the next weekend but I would never again run out at Highbury for Arsenal in Division One. For the rest of the season I was stuck in the reserves while anxiously thinking about my position with the club.

On the Monday after the Bolton match I was called up to Mr Crayston's office. He told me that Cardiff City would like to talk to me about a move back to South Wales. I agreed to a meeting and a day or so later I was in the company of Cardiff City director Fred Dewey and their manager Trevor Morris who had travelled down to London for the talks. I had discussed the situation with Glen and while she didn't want to leave London she left it to me to come to a decision.

The two gentlemen from Cardiff told me how much they would like to see me playing for the City but as the Bluebirds were well down Division Two after being relegated the previous season, it was not a move that really appealed to me at that stage in my career. When they could see my reluctance at making the move from Highbury, Mr Dewey shocked me by saying that if I signed for Cardiff he would make sure that I was in the Wales squad for the World Cup finals in Sweden at the end of the season. Only a few days earlier Wales had won a place in the Finals after beating Israel in a play-off.

Those words were like a red rag to a bull for me. There was no way I was going to accept what I classed to be a bribe from anyone, and I politely told them that I didn't want to leave Arsenal. I had no desire to cause trouble so when I was asked by Mr Crayston of the outcome of the talks I just said that my wife and I were settled in London and we preferred not to move away. That was the official reason that was eventually given out in a press statement as word had already gone around that Cardiff City were in talks with me.

In any case it was a viable reason as all our friends were in London. I hadn't lived in South Wales since before I went to do my national service and apart from that we were just getting the garden of our house into the shape we wanted. So it was back to reserve team football, albeit in front of 10-15,000 crowds.

Predictably, I was not named in the Wales squad going to Sweden in June even though I was perfectly fit and regularly knocking in the goals in the reserves. Perhaps the biggest selection shock was Cardiff City's inside forward Ron Hewitt. Ron joined the Bluebirds for the start of the 1957-58 season from Wrexham and played just two years and 70 games before returning to North Wales. After my dealings with Cardiff I often wondered whether there was more to that transfer than was ever told. He won all his five caps while at Ninian Park with his last one coming against Brazil in the World Cup quarter-final. He was never selected for Wales after moving back to Wrexham.

I wasn't the only one in the Tapscott household to have foot trouble about that time as Glen had to go in to hospital to have some work done on her big toe. It had been causing her discomfort for some time and needed to be sorted out. As soon as our pals from Covent Garden knew she was in hospital they flooded her room with flowers with new bouquets arriving every day. It was a lovely gesture from lovely people.

At the end of a season in which we finished in a very poor 12th place, mainly as a result of conceding 85 league goals, Mr Crayston did the honourable thing and resigned. He had been with Arsenal for 25 years in various capacities.

I don't think he was given the support and backing that other Arsenal managers have enjoyed and I know that he was very disappointed with the stance taken by the Arsenal board in regards to the recruiting of new players. He had regularly asked for money to improve the side but met with a blank wall each time. Arsenal's transfer policy at the time was to ask the selling club what fee they required for a particular player they were interested in. Once they were given that figure they held a board meeting to decide if the player was indeed worth that amount. If they felt it was too high, they took the matter no further.

Mr Crayston was very keen on signing my Wales team-mate Cliff Jones from Swansea Town but the Swans opening price was too high according to the Arsenal directors and instead he was transferred to our north London rivals Spurs who were more than ready to pay the asking fee.

Before Mr Crayston left the club however I was offered, and accepted, a new contract to cover the 1958-59 season.

There was talk that Joe Mercer would be coming to take over and that was a prospect I was really hoping would happen but it never came to fruition. Instead, Arsenal appointed their former goalkeeper, George Swindin to take over the reigns in readiness for the start of the new season and that was the beginning of the end of my time at the club.

Mr Swindin came from non-league side Peterborough United where he had achieved a couple of cup giant-killing feats that brought him to the public eye. In a very short time he had decided on who he wanted to remain at the club and who he was prepared to see off. One by one players began leaving as new faces arrived because unlike Jack Crayston, he had been given money by the board to spend. Out went former Cardiff player Mike Tiddy to Brighton, Cliff Holton was sold to Watford after 11 years service at Highbury, and I was told of interest in me for a second time from Cardiff City. When I was omitted from the pre-season tour party that went to Switzerland, I knew my time with Arsenal was coming to a close.

Yet I was in no hurry to leave Highbury. Glen and I were very happy living in London and I knew that given a bit of luck I could win my place back in the first team.

That all changed however when the list of names for Switzerland was pinned up on the notice board and I wasn't among those making the trip. Nothing had really gone right for me since that cartilage operation and yet I desperately wanted the chance to show the new manager what I could still do. Just because I finished the season in the reserves didn't mean I wasn't giving 100% in every game because that was the only way I could play. I never once thought of myself as a failure at Highbury and was willing to fight for my place and still take all the knocks and bruises that seemed to be coming my way. I decided to bide my time until the lads came back from overseas and then go in to see Mr Swindin.

When they returned, it was made clear to me by the manager that I was no longer going to be part of the first team and that it would be in both our interests if I moved elsewhere. Cardiff City had been back on the telephone to Arsenal asking about my availability so I decided to find out what they had to offer.

11

HOMEWARD BOUND

I thought I had always got on fairly well with George Swindin but he was determined to make a number of changes at the club and it was obvious that my face didn't fit. I had never caused any trouble for the Arsenal but when a new manager comes in and says you are free to go then that's usually it.

I let him know that if Cardiff City were still interested then I was prepared to meet with them and see what they had to offer. The Arsenal office telephoned the Cardiff club and a meeting was arranged at Ninian Park for Friday, 19 September, 1958.

Glen and I talked it over for hours and hours as we were very undecided what to do. Leaving Highbury would be a big wrench as we were very happy in London and even on the train from Paddington to South Wales that Friday morning we still poured over the pros and cons of leaving the capital. I wanted Glen to be with me at the meeting in Cardiff because it was such an important decision to make at this time in our lives.

When the train pulled in to Cardiff General Station I was delighted to see an old friend waiting for us on the platform. It was Bill Jones who was now acting manager of Cardiff City, the same Bill Jones who had taken me in the opposite direction when I left Barry for Arsenal almost five years earlier.

In July, Trevor Morris, the previous City manager, had accepted a position as manager of Swansea Town and Bill was appointed to the Cardiff job in a temporary capacity. It was Trevor Morris who had made the trip to Highbury for the transfer talks that I had turned down earlier in the year.

Bill welcomed us to Cardiff and the first thing we did on leaving the railway station was to visit one of the many restaurants in the city centre where the three of us enjoyed an excellent lunch. It was good to talk about old times with Bill and hear his plans for the future of Cardiff City. With lunch over it was then down to business and we went the short distance to Ninian Park by car and then straight into the manager's office. He explained to me exactly what the terms of their offer would be – £20 during the season and £18 in the summer – but he also told me that prior to signing a contract I would be required to take a rigorous medical examination. 'We know you have had a cartilage operation and we want to make sure that you can stand the strain of regular football,' he said.

There was no point in Glen waiting at Ninian Park until I returned so she came with me when I was taken to the Royal Infirmary by the club's medical officer John Evans. A specialist was waiting there to give me a number of tests on my knee after which he certified that there was nothing wrong whatsoever with my fitness.

In actual fact, while I was on my own with the specialist he told me that I could have trouble in the future with my left leg as he had found that it was a bit arthritic. 'Cardiff have only instructed me to report on your right knee after the cartilage operation so I will say nothing to them about the other knee.'

As it happened, I had never had any trouble with my left leg and never did throughout the rest of my career. I was never the slightest bit worried about the outcome of the medical as before the start of the season at Highbury our fitness levels were all checked and mine was as good as anyone's at the club.

Back to the ground in Sloper Road and the contract was placed before me but before I signed I wanted a final word with Glen in private to satisfy myself that she was happy with the move. We were allowed to spend a few minutes in a side room and we came to the decision that with the death of her father and with my dad being unwell, it was a good time to come back to South Wales. Glen's mam was living on her own in Barry and although all our friends were in London, we agreed that we would take a chance on a move to Cardiff. As Glen rightly said at the time, if we are going to have to make a move, it would be better to come back home rather than move further away and have to make all new friends again in a strange area.

On the football side, the City had only recently been relegated from Division One so there was every chance that I would soon be back playing in the top division.

Added to that of course was the fact that I would be playing once again for Bill Jones, a man I respected a great deal. Under George Swindin at Arsenal I was never going to get an opportunity as I obviously didn't fit in with his plans.

I was told that a fee of £10,000 had been agreed with Arsenal. It was also explained to me that Cardiff had started the season in poor form. They had gained only five points from the first eight games and were lying close to the bottom of the division. What was also said however was that they were aiming to regain their place in the top flight as soon as possible.

Bill said that he would be delighted if the club finished around halfway in the table as he regarded the season as a survival campaign.

He also had some more surprising news when he told me of further transfer developments at the club. 'You will not be the only new signing as we have also agreed a deal with Sunderland for the services of Don Revie, although there are still one or two matters to be sorted out as far as that transfer is concerned.' Middlesbrough were also in for Revie but at the end of the day he decided not to go anywhere and stayed at Sunderland until moving to Leeds United just before Christmas.

I was convinced that the club had ambition so at about 3.30 pm on Friday afternoon I signed for Cardiff City and a few minutes later I went out with my new manager to watch the lads completing their work-out.

I was surprised to find my old Arsenal team-mate Brian Walsh training on his own while the other forwards were practising a few routines. I asked Mr Jones, for now it was back to Mr Jones, or Boss, as he was my manager, why Walshy wasn't over there with the other lads and he said Brian had not been at his best in the last few games. Straightaway I told him that if he put him on the wing outside me I would see that he received plenty of ball and together we would open up the opposition defences. We knew how each other played and it was sure to pay dividends for the team. After the lads finished training I was introduced to all of them and I had the feeling that they were delighted to have me at the club.

When I went back into the club office I received a call from BBC Wales inviting me to their studios in Broadway where I opened the early evening news with the words – 'Hello, I'm Derek Tapscott'. After the main news of the day I was then interviewed about my move to Cardiff which had caused a great deal of excitement around the area. It seems that Arsenal Football Club still had something of an aura even in South Wales and my signing made all the local and national papers the following day.

On signing for the City I received a cheque in the sum of £1,070. This was made up of £750 benefit for five years service at Highbury plus £300 transfer bonus and a £20 signing on fee. Hardly a fortune even in those days but nevertheless a handy little sum to help soften the blow of dropping down a division.

There was no time to relax. Glen and I stayed the night at

her mam's house in Barry and a car was sent to collect me at lunchtime on the Saturday as Grimsby Town were the visitors to Ninian Park. Players had to be inside the ground at least one hour before kick-off and once inside I was delighted to find that Mr Jones had selected Daisy at outside right with me inside him. Before that however I was very happy to sign loads of autographs for the young lads who had gathered at the main gate to catch sight of any of the players as they made their way into the ground. I lost count of the number of times I was slapped on the back by the fans as I slowly made my way in through the players entrance.

The full City side on my debut that day was: Ron Nicholls; Alec Milne and Derrick Sullivan; Steve Gammon who was a 17 year-old also making his debut, Danny Malloy and Colin Baker at half back, while up front alongside me and Brian were Joe Bonson, Ron Hewitt and Brian Jenkins.

Steve lived in the Mumbles and was still working during the week as an apprentice. He only came to Ninian Park on Fridays and trained alone during the week. He could have been a great player.

One worrying note I found out while talking to the lads as we were preparing ourselves for the start was that Danny Malloy, captain for the day in place of the injured Ron Stitfall, was the only member of the team still to be playing in the same position since the start of the season and this was the ninth match.

It was a strange feeling running out at Ninian Park in the famous blue shirts but the home supporters gave me a marvellous welcome. In Division One with the Arsenal I knew most of the opposition players but Grimsby's side were completely unknown to me, in any case, I hardly knew my own side. The only player I had met before training the previous day was Derrick Sullivan who was also a Wales international, and Brian Walsh.

Once the whistle went all that was forgotten and it wasn't

long before Daisy had whipped over a cross which bounced around in their six yard box but just as I moved in a defender hacked the ball clear.

We went ahead very early in the match when their keeper failed to hold my shot and Joe Bonson had a tap-in. I also had a hand in our second goal soon after when Brian Jenkins sent over a high cross and as I moved in on their goalkeeper he took his eye off the ball and it hit the far post and bounced in. We went in at half-time 3-0 up as Ron Hewitt raced on to a Walsh pass to net with a low shot and when he scored another as soon as we returned from our cup of tea, the points were in the bag. They pulled one back but it was a great start to my new life as a Bluebird.

The crowd was around 15,000, about the same as would be at Highbury to watch a reserve match.

On the Sunday after the game it was back to our home in New Southgate, London as we had all the packing to do in readiness for a move back to South Wales. Arsenal were very good to us and said that we could stay in the club house for as long as was necessary. They also allowed me to continue training at Highbury and for that I was most grateful. The lads welcomed me back and wished me all the best at my new club. They even made sure I continued training alongside the Arsenal first team.

After training each day, Glen and I began collecting up our possessions and putting them in crates ready for despatch to Wales. When Friday arrived, we were back on the Paddington-Cardiff train as there was an important match on the Saturday at Anfield against Liverpool. I will never forget that it was against Liverpool that I made my debut for Arsenal. They were a lucky club for me then and would remain lucky for me while I was with the City. We stayed the night at Glen's mam's as we would do every weekend until we found our own house and early on Saturday morning I travelled to Liverpool with the rest of the lads.

When we arrived at Anfield a few of us walked out on to the pitch to get a feel of the place and then something happened that had I known about it before, it could well have changed my career completely. As I was looking around the ground I heard a voice shout out, 'Tappy, where were you last Friday night?'

I turned to see who was shouting and there was the Liverpool keeper Tommy Younger. I had first met Tommy when playing in Glasgow for Wales against Scotland and we always had a bit of banter during games. I walked over to him and asked what he meant about last Friday night.

'You were supposed to come over to Ashton Gate where we were playing Bristol City to discuss a move to Liverpool. The directors were waiting for you.' I told him that I never knew anything about a meeting so he called over a smart looking gentleman who was standing on the touchline and introduced him as a director of the Liverpool Football Club. He confirmed that they had indeed contacted Arsenal on the Friday, the very same day I had travelled to Cardiff to meet Bill Jones, and offered £20,000 for me. Arsenal then telephoned Cardiff in order to let me know of Liverpool's interest but somehow or other I was never given the message.

When I told Glen about it later that weekend she agreed with me that although as a matter of courtesy it would have been worth meeting the Liverpool officials, at that point in my career a move to Cardiff was probably a better bet. At that time of course, Liverpool were not the force they became under Bill Shankly. Don't forget that the season we beat them 3-0 on my debut for Arsenal they were relegated to Division Two after finishing in bottom place.

Well there was no way the side could be changed after the win over Grimsby so it was the same eleven who did duty that afternoon against the Reds.

It was that day I realised how clever Danny Malloy was as

captain. He surprised everyone, and in particular the Liverpool players, by opting to play into a stiff breeze in the first half after winning the toss. It seemed to be the wrong decision when Alan Banks, who was a 19 year old apprentice plumber, put his side ahead in the opening minutes but Danny knew what he was doing. We allowed Liverpool to run themselves out and then started putting the pressure on. I was unlucky with a couple of shots that struck the bar leaving my old mate Tommy Younger floundering but then Joe Bonson and Ron Hewitt scored and we had the upper hand. It was then that they started the physical stuff and it became a bit of a roughhouse as they kicked any Cardiff player who came near. Brian Jenkins needed treatment on the touchline after one bad tackle and then I needed repairs following a clash with Ronnie Moran which left me on the grass with a dead arm. Poor Brian Walsh ended up on his backside every time he made a run down the wing. But we kept our composure while Liverpool had completely lost theirs and deservedly won 2-1 for our first away win of the season and only their second home defeat in almost two years. Danny was superb at the back and he completely shut out Billy Liddell who was their main danger man. There was no excuse for Liverpool's dirty play even though they were losing at home.

It was back to the routine of living in London during the week and training at Highbury and while this kept my fitness levels up, it was little help in getting to know my new team-mates although it didn't stop me from shouting instructions at everyone during the games.

Middlesbrough were next to visit Ninian Park and on the Saturday of the match, Danny Malloy came up to me and said in his strong Scottish accent, 'You do enough talking on the pitch, so why don't you take over as captain. You have the experience after playing in Division One and you keep everyone on their toes during the games.' It was a great gesture but I had already realised after just two outings with Cardiff that Danny was a far better captain than I would ever be and I told him so.

Leading Boro's line was none other than Brian Clough and he had a couple of half chances but generally Danny had the beating of him. We won 3-2 in front of a 20,000 crowd after being 3-0 up in torrential rain but after three games I was still without a goal. That would come the following week against Ipswich but it would also signal the end of our winning run as the Suffolk side won 2-1. I had opened the scoring when Joe Bonson pulled down a long pass from Colin Baker and whipped the ball into the centre. I raced through the middle and flicked it inside the near post but Ipswich were a good side and probably deserved to win.

We put together another little winning run of three matches and then came a visit to Craven Cottage, another ground that I was familiar with. A Brian Walsh goal was not enough and Fulham won 2-1 but it was a brilliant display by the lads. The difference between the sides was their keeper Tony Macedo who had an incredible game and stopped just about everything we threw at him. A very young George Cohen was at full back for them and on the wing was Graham Leggatt, the Scottish international, and he had a good game.

I had fantastic news at the start of the next week when I was included in the Wales side to play England at Villa Park to win my 13th cap. It had been a long time coming as I had not been selected since being injured against East Germany in Leipzig nearly 18 months previously.

In our next match against table toppers Sheffield Wednesday we were 2-0 down but fought back to earn a 2-2 draw. I was in the wars that day and had to leave the field for treatment after being clattered by their centre half, Peter Swan. While I was off the field receiving attention, the referee stopped the game to ask two policemen to stand behind the Wednesday goal to prevent orange peel being thrown at their keeper. Despite hobbling about I managed to poke the ball in for the equaliser after Brian Jenkins had pulled one back.

I was fit enough to take my place in the Wales side the following Wednesday and partnering me at inside right for his debut was Dai Ward, a Barry boy playing at Bristol Rovers who had also played for Barry Town before doing his national service.

It was good to meet up with my old Arsenal team-mates Jack Kelsey and Dave Bowen but John Charles was missing because Juventus wanted him for a friendly against Arsenal on the evening of the International.

There was a bit of a fuss beforehand when the English FA asked the Welsh FA to play the game under the Villa Park floodlights instead of kicking off at 2.00 pm. The Welsh FA refused, saying that international matches should be played in daylight and not under artificial conditions.

That decision was to help Jack Kelsey as he wanted to play for Wales in the afternoon and then race to London to appear for Arsenal in the evening.

The Wales squad were based in Droitwich Spa. We travelled to our quarters on the Monday and trained morning and afternoon in dense fog at Droitwich Town's ground on the Tuesday. After training we all went for brine baths.

Once again team selection was held up when Phil Woosnam was confined to bed on the morning of the match and Cardiff's Brian Jenkins was called up as a precaution.

Fortunately Phil, who was with West Ham at the time, recovered to take his place in the starting line-up.

We took a shock lead in the opening minutes when Colin McDonald failed to hold a shot from Dai Ward and I ran in and poked the loose ball into the net. Dave Bowen then fell heavily and injured his arm and leg which resulted in him being a passenger out on the wing for the remainder of the game. This meant that Dai had to drop back into Dave's wing half spot and I was left up front on my own. England went looking for the equaliser and Ronnie Clayton banged a shot against the post before Peter Broadbent lobbed Jack in the closing minutes of the first half to make it 1-1.

Ivor Allchurch then came into the match in a big way and he left a couple of defenders standing before whacking the ball past McDonald to put us ahead again but our lead didn't last long as Broadbent headed his second goal to complete the scoring. It was a great performance from the ten men and if Dave Bowen had been fit we could well have beaten England.

Straight after the match Jack caught a train to London and he was in time to play for Arsenal in their 3-1 win over Juventus. Charlo scored the goal for the Italian side.

Towards the end of the year, the Cardiff directors had seen what a good job Mr Jones was doing and officially made him manager. Within a matter of weeks he brought former City player Wilf Grant to the club as coach. Wilf had been combining playing with managing Welsh League side Llanelly.

Mr Jones was trying to get a few players out so that he could bring new ones in and Ron Hewitt was offered a move to Mansfield but he refused to go and they signed reserve team player Cliff Nugent instead.

A visit to Sunderland was always going to be a tough trip but playing the match in dense fog made it a lottery. The floodlights had to be switched on at the start otherwise you couldn't see more than a dozen yards. Making his debut for them was little Ernie Taylor who had signed from Manchester United the day before. Somehow we overcame the conditions and I slid the first goal past their keeper Peter Wakeham and Joe Bonson settled it in the second half. Derrick Sullivan blotted Taylor out of the match but it was difficult to see anything in that fog, particularly with the

white ball. In the dying seconds Taylor was brought down in
our penalty area but Billy Elliott's spot kick went high over
the bar, much to Ron Nicholls relief.

By now Glen and I had packed everything and to be fair
to Arsenal we decided to put all our belongings and furniture
in storage in Cardiff and move in with her mam until such
time as we found a house we liked, and could afford. I also
decided it would be a good time to use my London contacts
and buy a car. My good friend Bob Silva helped me as he
knew a dealer in Warren Street, London and he arranged a
good deal for a white Ford 375. It had a bench seat in the
front and a column change and was a big car. I felt at home
in it because it was like driving a tank. It was only a couple of
months old and cost me about £400. That was the second car
Bob had found for me. The first one I had checked out at
Ford's in Cardiff and they discovered a few defects and
warned me against buying it so I drove it back to London and
had the 375 instead.

It didn't take me long to get in trouble with the law over
the car. I parked it outside Glen's house one Friday night and
even put the parking light on that worked from the cigarette
lighter. At about midnight when we were in bed, there was a
knock on the door and it was a policeman. He wanted to
know whose car it was and I had to find all the papers and my
driving licence. He then told me that I was parked facing the
oncoming traffic and that I should be the other way round.
He made me get changed and go out and turn the car around
to face the other way. That was the first time the Tapscott
name wasn't any help to me.

After viewing a few properties we found one in Cog Road,
Sully that we really liked. We were given a price of £3,900
which was about the limit we could afford, and I left my
name with the agent who would arrange a viewing. The
following day when we rang up to find out the time of the
appointment we were told that a mistake had been made

with the price of the house and that it was really £4,500. I still believe to this day that when they found out that it was Derek Tapscott interested in buying the property they upped the price. So that was the second time being a Tapscott was no help to me.

We eventually found a lovely house in the north of Cardiff close to Whitchurch Golf Club in November and moved in on 23 December, 1958. We were going to leave it until after Christmas but Bob Silva wanted to come and stay over the Christmas holiday with his family and he had been so good to us when we were in London that we couldn't refuse. He turned up in a Bentley with his wife, kids and a maid and they all mucked in to help us sort everything out and even put our curtains up for us.

Fortunately the matches over the holiday period were against Bristol City and on Boxing Day we won 3-2 at Ashton Gate and in the return at Ninian Park the following day we won 1-0 to make it an even better Christmas all round.

We had a few good wins but then suffered a big shock when we went down 5-1 at Grimsby for our heaviest defeat of the season. Harry Knowles, a new signing from Worcester, came in at centre forward and Brayley Reynolds was at outside right in place of the injured Brian Walsh. Nothing went right for us and we were well beaten by a side we had trounced 4-1 on my debut earlier in the season.

By then I had already been in to see Mr Jones as I was worried about my lack of goals. I told him that I couldn't understand it. I was top scorer for two seasons at Arsenal not so long ago yet I had only scored four times since coming to Cardiff.

He was very sympathetic and told me, 'Don't worry – you are doing the job you were bought for. Let me do the worrying while you just go out and play football.'

Those words made me feel a little better although I still believed that the Cardiff fans thought I had lost my touch in front of goal. It was nothing to do with fitness as I was as fit as ever and still able to take the knocks. Still, the chat with Mr Jones paid early dividends.

Next up were Liverpool and after two wins in two matches against them I did not want to spoil that record. In any case, after their rough stuff at Anfield we all thought we had a score to settle with them. They arrived at Ninian Park on the back of eight successive victories and were third in Division Two but we were up for it. I linked up with Walshy and when his cross came in I met it with a sweet volley past my old mate Tommy Younger in the Liverpool goals. It was one of the best goals of my career. Suddenly it all came back to me and when another Walsh cross came over I chipped Younger for my second and the points were already in the bag. Brayley Reynolds made sure with a third goal late in the second half and they went back to Merseyside a well-beaten outfit.

Our FA Cup run didn't last very long. We beat Plymouth Argyle 3-0 at their place but in round four we travelled to Carrow Road to meet giant-killers Norwich City who were a Third Division side in those days. No way should we have lost as we were the better side but two late goals by Terry Bly and we were knocked out 3-2. Norwich went on to reach the semi-finals that season.

A few weeks later came my first taste of a Cardiff-Swansea derby. Even in those days beating Swansea was a must for all Cardiff players and fans alike, especially at Ninian Park as there was no love lost between the clubs. The atmosphere was very much like the Spurs-Arsenal derbies I played in. Included in their side was Mel Charles, Ray Daniel and Len Allchurch, Ivor's brother who was out on the wing, while at centre forward was Colin Webster who had recently signed for the club from Manchester United.

It was a wet day and the pitch became a gluepot with proper football out of the question. They were given a very dubious penalty and Mel Nurse scored to give them their first win and very first goal in a league game at Ninian Park. We had revenge in the return at the Vetch when we won 3-1 and Nurse helped us to victory by scoring an own goal. That was another wet day and the Vetch resembled a lake when we arrived at the ground but it dried out enough for the referee to agree to start the match.

I thought my leg was broken in that game after one particularly bad challenge. My shinpad was split in half by the force and John Evans, the team doctor, said that my leg would have been broken but for that protection. In all I was off the field for about half an hour in the first half receiving treatment.

I chipped in with a couple more goals in the next few games and that was enough for the Wales selectors to keep me in the team to play Northern Ireland in Belfast on 22 April, 1959. On the same day City were meeting Sunderland at Ninian Park and while I was in the Emerald Isle with team-mate Derrick Sullivan, Ron Hewitt and Brian Walsh were scoring to give the lads a 2-1 win.

Unfortunately, it wasn't as good for us in Ireland as we were pretty poor and ended up well-beaten, 4-1. Leading our line in his one and only appearance for Wales was Tony Rowley who played for Tranmere Rovers in Division Three while in goal was Vic Rouse of Crystal Palace who played in Division Four. Rouse had been brought in because Jack Kelsey had been injured playing for the Arsenal. The selection of Rowley owed more to the club he played for rather than his ability. When it was realised at the last minute that Juventus would not release John Charles for our game, the selectors tried first for Dai Ward and then for Roy Vernon but both players were on the injured list. With time running out and the boat just about ready to sail to Belfast from Liverpool, Rowley was roped in from nearby Tranmere and he turned up just before we were due to sail.

We arrived in Belfast at 8.00 am and had a full day's training before resting up in the evening. Mel Charles was absent from the squad because he had just made the move from Swansea Town to Arsenal for a £40,000 fee and to the annoyance of the Welsh selectors he had forgotten to insert a clause in his contract to make sure that he would be released for international matches. Arsenal had a friendly against Glasgow Rangers at Highbury the day before our game and George Swindin wanted Mel to play for them in that match. The selectors in their wisdom decided that Mel could not play on consecutive days so left him out of the squad. Swindin had a lot to say about it in the papers that week. 'If a player cannot play two games in two days at this stage of the season then he is not worth his £20 a week.'

We were up against an experienced Irish side led by my old friend Danny Blanchflower and the absence of so many of our leading players turned out to be very costly. Rouse had a poor debut in goals and his uncertainty spread to the other members of the defence and Jimmy McIlroy and Peter McParland took full advantage. Before we knew it we were 4-0 down but it could have been better with a little bit of luck. Ivor Allchurch fisted one in and we thought we had got away with it but the linesman had spotted the handball. To this day I reckon I had a perfectly good goal ruled out when I dived to head in a cross from Terry Medwin. I'm sure it was over the line before Harry Gregg clawed it back. When I spoke to him about it after the game he just grinned and said 'Some you win Tappy, and some you lose.'

I managed a consolation goal two minutes from time when Tony Rowley slipped a short pass in to me inside the area and at last I beat Gregg by firing into the corner of the net. Little did I know then that the game in Belfast would be my last in a Welsh shirt. I would have preferred to have ended on a winning note although I did have the satisfaction of scoring in each of my last two appearances.

On the league front I salvaged a point with our goal in the 1-1 draw at Sheffield United in the last game of the season and three days later I was the proud owner of a Welsh Cup winners medal after we beat Lovells Athletic 2-0 at Somerton Park, Newport.

I finished my first season with the Bluebirds with ten league goals which I thought was a little disappointing from a personal point of view. However, the club had ended up in ninth spot to set a standard that would have to be improved the following season if we wanted to achieve promotion. When I joined in the September the team was struggling but I could tell right away that the players were hungry for success. There were young players coming through like Steve Gammon and Graham Moore and with a good sound defence we genuinely believed that we had a good chance of making Division One very quickly.

12

BACK TO THE BIG TIME

During the summer I relaxed while Glen busied herself in the garden. I also managed to get in a round or two of golf. The two of us also used the time to get to know our whereabouts in Cardiff as the area was still quite new to us. We also stayed for a few days with my sisters in Willesden and Oxford.

In no time at all it was back in for training and the start of what would turn out to be a momentous season for the club. Mr Jones only signed two new players and they were both forwards. Steve Mokone, known at the club as Kalamazoo, came from a Dutch side and Johnny Watkins arrived from Bristol City. Leaving Ninian Park were Brayley Reynolds who went to archrivals Swansea, and Ron Hewitt who went back to Wrexham after only two seasons at Ninian Park.

Most of the lads had some weight to sweat off but I never had any trouble like that. I only wished that I could have put a little bit of weight on. Derrick Sullivan suffered more than most when training resumed. He used to wear a waterproof tracksuit while he was training in an effort to shed those unwanted pounds. Derrick enjoyed a drink and the summer months were a big temptation. None of the players would go out for the evening with Derrick because he could drink them under the table. But he never let that interfere with his football and he was probably the best utility player ever to appear for Cardiff City. Hardly any of the other lads drank. If I went out, all I would have was a half of Mackeson, a bit like a Guinness, and that was only because it was supposed to be good for me.

In those days there was always a Firsts against Seconds the week before the season started and as young Graham Moore scored four times in that match he was included for the opener against Liverpool.

As so often happens, the first day of the season was boiling hot and we kept the temperature high by scoring after five minutes through Kalamazoo. I had managed to work my way through and when Bert Slater pushed my shot away little Steve was on hand to score on his debut. I knew exactly how he was feeling after scoring on my debut for Arsenal against Liverpool almost five years previously.

In an amazing turn-round, we found ourselves 2-1 down at half time without a Liverpool player scoring. Poor Danny Malloy, who had a bit of a reputation for scoring 'Ogies', sliced two clearances past Graham Vearncombe inside seven minutes and we were up against it although we were much the better side. Golden Boy Moore levelled straight after half time with a close range shot and then a Johnny Watkins thunderbolt gave us a 3-2 lead which we kept to the end of the game.

Johnny Watkins was great to play with. During the season we would practice corner routines together and it paid off on several occasions. He certainly had a powerful shot on him. Young Graham would go on to get better and better although he was not a robust player and he didn't like getting stuck in but he could pass the ball with the best of them. He always wore number nine when he was in the team while I had number eight, but numbers didn't bother me.

We beat Middlesbrough 2-0 in midweek but then I was injured at the Valley where Charlton took advantage to beat us 2-1. That put me out of action for the next five games and after playing in the 4-1 home defeat by Rotherham United I was also forced to miss the next two games.

When I returned to action for the first team against Leyton Orient in the middle of October it coincided with our best display of the season. We won 5-1, I managed to score twice for my first goals of the season, and we moved into second place in the division behind Aston Villa. Before the game the teams lined up for a minute's silence in memory of Sir Herbert Merrett, the Cardiff City president who had died a few days previously.

My return had come too late for the Wales selectors and I was not included in the squad for the match against England in Cardiff on 17 October, the same day City played at Huddersfield Town. We travelled north without Derrick Sullivan, Alan Harrington and Graham Moore who were on Wales duty.

Despite being under strength, the lads who came in did very well and we claimed all the points with a 1-0 victory. A Johnny Watkins centre went to Joe Bonson whose first time shot was pushed out by Ray Wood. The loose ball came my way and I was able to stroke it into an empty net.

Huddersfield should have equalised in the second half when Denis Law fell down in the box after a challenge from Danny Malloy. Law stepped up to take the spot kick but Graham Vearncombe guessed right and saved at the foot of the post. During the match Steve Gammon, who always seemed to be in the wars, had to go off the field after suffering a blow in the face but we battled away with ten men until he returned.

Meanwhile at Cardiff, a late goal by Graham Moore gave Wales a 1-1 draw against England.

The goals were now starting to come for me and I was pleased with the one I netted against Ipswich in the next match. I gathered a long ball from Johnny Watkins, rounded their centre half Andy Nelson, and as Roy Bailey came out of goal towards me I flicked it over his head. I caught up with the ball as it was rolling towards the by-line and hooked it just inside the post.

Swansea were next at Ninian Park and they were confident of winning as they had been doing reasonably well. Colin Webster dished out the rough stuff all through the game and put his name on the scoresheet with a close range header but by then we were two up through Derrick Sullivan and Joe Bonson. Danny Malloy also had the ball in the net in the closing minutes but the referee disallowed it because he reckoned I was offside. I took a lot of flak from Danny after the match because of that decision.

A trip to Brighton was memorable only for the fact that it was good to meet up with Mike Tiddy once again. After a 2-2 draw we had a long chat about our time at Arsenal.

We had gone 11 games unbeaten when we visited Villa Park to take on league leaders Aston Villa. There was a massive crowd of 54,000 watching as Villa won 2-0 with one of their goals coming from former City player, Gerry Hitchens.

To stay in the promotion race we knew we had to get something from our next game which was at Liverpool. A few days before the match Bill Shankly was appointed as manager. It was one way traffic for the whole 90 minutes. Brian Walsh took Ronnie Moran to the cleaners and Danny Malloy blotted out Dave Hickson their number nine.

We turned them over 4-0, I scored two of them and Johnny Watkins and Walshy added the others. It was such a good display that we heard on the grapevine that Shanks reckoned it was one of the best performances he had ever seen. After the match, Ronnie Moran told me that Cardiff were certain of promotion if they maintained that form. That gave us the double over Liverpool to add to the double of the previous year. The Reds were still good enough to finish in third place in the division at the end of the season.

For me personally it was a fifth win against them in five games and I had scored six goals.

We were now scoring goals for fun and with Walsh and Watkins on the wing and Joe Bonson, Graham Moore and me inside, we were more than a match for most defences.

There was a slight setback in the Third Round of the FA Cup when we were beaten 2-0 at Ninian Park by Port Vale who were a mid-table Division Three side. It was the first time we had failed to score that season at home, but at least it allowed us to concentrate on the league.

There was a funny incident at Ashton Gate when we played against Bristol City. I cracked a shot past their keeper and it hit the stanchion behind the goal and came straight back out onto the field while the goalie was still on his back. Graham Moore raced across to me and shook my hand so together we ran back to the centre circle as if it was a goal. The poor keeper didn't know whether it had gone in or not. Unfortunately, the referee had a clear sight of the incident and awarded a goal kick much to the keeper's relief. It didn't make any difference to the result however as we romped it 3-0.

Results kept going our way and in the February, we beat Hull City 3-2 at Ninian Park to go top of the league. It was a hard-earned victory as Alec Milne, our Scottish left back was a passenger out on the wing for most of the game. Alec was a good lad and an excellent full back. If he had been playing with a Scottish club I am sure he would have won a full cap. As it was, he had to be content with an Under-23 appearance while playing with the City.

The game after that will long be remembered for Joe Bonson's diving header. We were playing Leyton Orient at Brisbane Road and it was 3-3 towards the closing minutes of the game. I chased down the right wing after a Brian Walsh pass and sent over a chest high cross. Joe had run down the middle and he launched himself at the ball and headed home while in mid air from around the penalty spot. There was an incredible photograph of a horizontal Joe in that weekend's Sunday papers.

Walshy was playing the best football of his career. He had found a confidence in his game because he knew the other members of the team respected his ability. And it was not only on the pitch that he was in demand because he was the unpaid financial adviser to nearly all the other lads at the club. His experience as an accountant made him a good choice to give advice to his mates and he was always ready to help where he could.

Two days before that match the club was forced to play a Welsh Cup tie against Swansea at the Vetch. Mr Jones requested that the game be postponed particularly as Cardiff were chasing promotion but the Welsh FA refused. So a reserve side was sent to play the Swans and they came away with a 2-1 win but not without cost. Colin Hudson was sent off for a foul, and then Steve Mokone and Swansea's Harry Griffiths were also dismissed after slinging mud at each other. Cardiff City were fined £350 and ordered to play their strongest side in future Welsh Cup games despite winning the match. This was to prove a ridiculous ruling by the out of touch Welsh FA as was proved the very next season.

We continued to pick up points and when Easter Saturday came we knew that two more would ensure promotion. The only problem was that our opponents were table-toppers Aston Villa. Over 50,000 crammed into Ninian Park to see the game in which we played in white shirts and shorts for a reason that escapes me.

We had Colin Hudson, known as Rock, in for the unfit Joe Bonson while Villa were without the injured Gerry Hitchens whose place was taken by Johnny Dixon. The Irish international Peter McParland was on the left wing.

It was a tough match with both sides afraid to make a

mistake as we all knew the high stakes. I went through the middle and was put flat on my face by Len Saward for a definite penalty but the referee waved play on. We scored the goal we needed quite early when Brian Walsh played a ball down the line to Rock and he crossed into the middle where Graham Moore hammered a great shot into the net past the diving Nigel Sims. We hung on to win 1-0 and secured promotion to Division One. After the game every City player appeared in the grandstand to be introduced to the crowd who had come onto the field at the end of the match. They covered just about every blade of grass. It was a fantastic achievement for the players and Mr Jones, and we celebrated in the dressing room after the match with bottles of champagne.

Unfortunately, after that win we seemed to take our foot off the pedal and instead of going on to win the league title, we fell away badly in our last three matches, only collected two points out of the six on offer, and ended up a point behind Villa with Liverpool eight points behind us in third place. Nevertheless, we were promoted, and I was on my way back to Division One where I wanted to be.

As a bonus for winning promotion the club went on a tour of East Germany but the border was closed before we reached it due to the American U2 spy plane incident and the trip had to be abandoned. Instead we went to Switzerland and played Division Two side Sunderland who were also on tour in Europe but it was a meaningless match which ended 0-0 and to be frank wasn't taken seriously by either side.

After the game all the players were in our hotel and we decided to buy the directors a drink as a gesture of goodwill for taking us on the trip. I found out what they wanted, as well as all the lads, ordered the drinks, and then put the cost of them on the club's tab. In fairness, they never moaned about it later on.

My golf was improving by leaps and bounds and during the summer I was lucky enough to win the Silver Putter at my club in Whitchurch.

13

PLAYING IN THE TOP FLIGHT

Everyone was back for pre-season training in high spirits. It was a gruelling start but I enjoyed all the runs, just as I had at the Arsenal.

Wilf Grant had us running out of the ground, up Leckwith Hill and back along Penarth Road before returning to Ninian Park. Another one of his tricks was to take us to Barry Island and on to the beach for sprinting and exercising. Running on sand is a real killer.

I would also do a bit of running on my own after training or perhaps in the early evening. I would run from my house up Thornhill to the top of Caerphilly Mountain.

Sometimes I would meet up with Alan Harrington and Colin Baker who also both lived locally. They regularly ran up the mountain. After meeting at the top we would go into the Traveller's Rest and enjoy a good chinwag and perhaps a half of shandy. Those were the days.

Every new trainer brings his own methods and Wilf was no exception. One idea however I brought to the club. At the Arsenal we were all issued with spikes as one session at Highbury would be speed work. When I was transferred to Cardiff I brought the spikes with me for training and most of the lads wanted a pair. In a surprise move, the club coughed up the money to equip everyone. On Fridays, after all the hard training had been done, we had 'Spikes Day' where all we did was sprints to help our speed off the mark. Most of the lads enjoyed that part of the training as it was all short bursts. After that we usually finished up with games of head tennis.

Our pre-season was completed with a trip to Holland in early August, a couple of weeks before our first league match. We played badly in the first game against DWS Amsterdam and then moved into Switzerland where we were beaten 4-3 by the Zurich Grasshoppers. Johnny Watkins scored a hat-trick against the Swiss side.

Mr Jones had made a few changes in personnel as he prepared for Division One football. I was disappointed to see my frontline partner Joe Bonson move to Scunthorpe but we did get Peter Donnelly in exchange. He would prove to be a big bustling bruiser of a centre forward who was never afraid to get stuck-in.

A lot of work had been carried out on the ground during the summer including the addition of floodlighting, though Ninian Park was one of the last grounds to have this facility installed.

Unfortunately, our opening game of the 1960-61 season was at one of my old stamping grounds, Craven Cottage, where we came up against Johnny Haynes.

We must have been running on adrenalin because we raced into a 2-0 lead through Walshy and Graham Moore. But Fulham found their legs in the second half and eventually held us to a 2-2 draw with Haynes bagging the equaliser.

Graham was a very polite young lad from the Valleys who would always listen to any bit of advice given to him. It seemed strange to me that I was giving advice and tips to the youngsters when just five years previously Tommy Lawton and Joe Mercer were giving me help. All the young lads were very respectful to the older pros at Cardiff, but don't forget, although I was a seasoned international and had played for five years with Arsenal in Division One, I was still only 28.

We had our first victory back in the top flight when I

scored to beat Preston 1-0 at Ninian Park and then we followed that with a superb 2-1 success at League Champions Burnley where once again I was on the scoresheet. The winner came from a Johnny Watkins piledriver in the dying seconds.

We failed to win any of our next four games as the standard of Division One began to hit home. Next up were Arsenal and I had been looking forward to this match since the fixtures came out although I never expected it to end in the way it did. I was very proud when I was made captain for the day and it couldn't have turned out better even though I almost had a scrap with George Swindin.

I desperately wanted to show him that he was wrong to get rid of me. They were without Tommy Docherty who had joined the club just as I was leaving. He had been injured in their last game against Birmingham and Gerry Ward deputised for him. My old mate Jack Kelsey was in goals and apart from a couple of newcomers, I knew all the rest of their lads.

We were really up for it that day. As far as the City boys were concerned, playing the likes of the Arsenal was what being in the top division was all about.

Steve Gammon and Rock Hudson started in place of the injured Derrick Sullivan and Brian Walsh, while Peter Donnelly was up front in place of Alan Durban.

Before the kick-off, an Arsenal fan dressed in red and white paraded around the pitch with a large banner saying, 'The Arsenal club welcome Cardiff City back to the First Division.' That was a nice touch which showed there was an affinity between the two teams.

It was a ding-dong struggle all through the match with neither side giving way. I managed to give Jack Kelsey a couple of digs to let him know I was still around and Peter Donnelly also had a go at him but there were no clearcut goal chances for either side. By half time Jack was in trouble having pulled a thigh muscle and he came out for the second half heavily strapped up. After another challenge from Peter, Jack wagged a finger at him as he was really suffering.

The winning goal came out of nothing. A harmless looking cross came in from Rock Hudson out on the right wing and I jumped up with Jack in an attempt to head the ball. It struck me somewhere on the arm and shot into the net. The Arsenal lads went mad when the referee signalled a goal. Jack said 'Go on, tell him you hit it in with your arm.' I told him that the referee had given a goal so it was a goal.

There was an unusual incident towards the end of the game. Arsenal full back Flint McCullough took off one of his boots and threw it over the touchline, finishing the match with one boot on and one off. When I spoke to him afterwards he said that he had blisters because the boots were fairly new.

I had a quick cup of tea with our lads at the end of the game and then went across to the visitors dressing room, knocked on the door, and when they saw it was me they let me in. None of the Arsenal boys were particularly happy at the result, or how it came about, but that was football and they were as pleased to see me as I was to see them. I was having a laugh and joke with Vic Groves and Gerry Ward when the door opened and in came George Swindin. He went absolutely ballistic when he saw me there.

'That is not the kind of thing you were taught at the Arsenal,' he said, referring to the alleged handball. 'I don't want your sort in here, you can get out now.'

I remained where I was next to Vic Groves, looked him in the eye and with a smile on my face reminded him that the referee gave a goal. The next moment he was starting to take his jacket off as though he was going to forcibly remove me. I had never seen him in such a rage as he was usually very controlled. Vic and Jack swiftly pushed me out of the door while a couple of other lads held Swindin back until I disappeared from view. I was glad to get away from that situation in one piece, but never dreamt that circumstances would mean that in the not-too-distant future I would once again come into contact with the same George Swindin.

We suffered a real blow in the next match when Graham Moore broke his leg at Newcastle and we were slaughtered 5-0.

The following midweek Zurich Grasshoppers came to Ninian Park in a match that officially opened the floodlights. It was a little taste of the European football that was to come in a few years time. Two other continental sides also came to Cardiff during the season. They were French side FC Biel and the Germans of FC Osnabruck. They were light relief from the pressures of Division One football.

Mr Jones felt that the side now needed a little extra craft out wide and so he went to West Brom and signed their left winger Derek Hogg for a fee in the region of £12,000. It was money well spent because Hoggy was a good player who could hold the ball and then use it to good advantage. I knew him from his days at the Albion. When he actually signed for the City he did it in front of the television cameras on a sports programme. He stayed with his wife at our house until the club organised accommodation for him. They were good company for the short time they spent with us.

Two days after signing he was in tremendous form against Leicester, one of his former clubs, and scored on his debut in a 2-1 win. The other goal came from Peter Donnelly who barged Gordon Banks into the net at the Canton Stand end.

Ron Nicholls was unhappy because he had lost his place in the first team to Graham Vearncombe and he now had Maurice Swan breathing down his neck. He decided to ask for a transfer and was put on the list by the club. After training one day he came to me and said, 'Tappy, I don't really want to go because this is the happiest club and best atmosphere that I have ever experienced in my career.' I told him to think carefully before making a move, and a week or so later he withdrew his request.

Manchester United came to Ninian Park at the end of November and that was a special moment for me as I hadn't played against them since facing the Busby Babes the weekend before the Munich crash.

The game was in doubt because of the torrential rain and the enclosure was flooded on the morning of the match. Fortunately, the rain stopped and the floodwater drained away making play possible.

It was Noel Cantwell's first game for United but Daisy took him to the cleaners. It was one of the best games he ever played for the City. He kept shouting for the ball because he knew he had the beating of Cantwell who had just joined United for a massive £30,000 fee from West Ham. For good measure he also gave Bill Foulkes a hard time on the other flank when he crossed over for a change of scenery. In fairness to United Dennis Viollett was injured early on and a passenger for most of the game but even with a full side there was no way they would have beaten us that day. When Dennis went down injured a cross came in, hit him while he was on the deck, and rolled towards our goal before being cleared. We won 3-0 with Hoggy scoring two and Brian Edgeley the other. I had a couple of chances that went begging but I will never forget Daisy's performance that day.

I had a belated Christmas present on Boxing Day when West Brom came to Ninian Park and I bagged a hat-trick, my first for Cardiff but my second in Division One.

We were called in for training on Christmas Eve, which was a Saturday, and it felt very strange training on the day normally set aside for a match.

Christmas Day was spent quietly at home, just the two of us.

Albion were in trouble at the bottom of the league but they put up a good fight. I scored early into the match but they fought back and equalised. We started putting on the pressure and a slip by their full back gave me the chance to nip in and put us ahead again at half time. The ground was very heavy and it was hard going all through the game but we stuck at it and I netted the third a few minutes from time.

The following day I was out of the house very early as we had a train to catch to take us to Birmingham for the return match. We drew 1-1 at the Hawthorns where Colin Baker, a steady player who could be relied upon at all times, scored his third goal in four matches.

We did the double over Burnley and after losing 2-1 at Nottingham Forest prepared to meet Manchester City at Ninian Park. It would be the fifth meeting of the season after the clubs needed three games to resolve a third round cup match which eventually went 2-0 in their favour in a second replay held at Highbury of all places.

Before that however there was the little matter of the Welsh Cup. We had been drawn at home to Knighton, a village side from mid-Wales and the game took place at Ninian Park on a Saturday set aside for the fourth round of the FA Cup. The Welsh FA in their wisdom had decreed that in all Welsh Cup matches Cardiff had to play their strongest side so it was the full Division One line-up that played against the amateurs. At first, the small crowd must have thought that it could be Knighton's day as I missed a good chance, Graham Moore shot wide, and then Brian Walsh hit a penalty well wide of the posts. But it was a false dawn for the villagers and by half time we were 7-0 up and Graham and I had already nabbed hat-tricks.

He took his tally up to four straight after the restart and the farce continued when I scored three more in quick succession even though we were now down to ten men after Alan Harrington left the field with two cracked ribs.

With the score at 12-0, I swapped places with Danny Malloy and went to centre half while he got one of the biggest cheers of the afternoon when he went up front and scored. Peter Donnelly netted his second and Brian Walsh and Derek Hogg took the score to an incredible 16-0 with the final goals. We genuinely felt sorry for the Knighton lads but we wanted to prove a point to the Welsh FA and that afternoon I think we did. On a personal basis, my six goals remain a record in one match for any Cardiff City player and I am very proud of that even though the opposition was so weak.

Back on the league scene and that game against Manchester City which finished 3-3 after we were leading 3-1. We would have taken both points but the heart went out of us after we saw what happened to young Steve Gammon. He was crunched by Denis Law right in front of the tunnel and suffered a compound fracture of the right leg. It was a very bad challenge from Law who was known to have a short fuse and Steve had been playing him out of the game.

I think Law had been frustrated as Steve had the better of him in our cup matches as well. Why he wasn't sent off I will never know. He was lucky the crowd didn't get on and lynch him as it happened quite close to the touchline and everyone in that area of the ground had a good view of Law going over the ball. Steve would never really recover from that tackle and his career was really over before it had begun. Everyone could hear the crack as Law went in. It was heartbreaking and took me back to my Arsenal debut when Joe Mercer, the oldest player on the field, broke his leg. Here I am in the same situation but where the youngest player on the field has now broken his leg. He went on to fracture the same leg twice more before finally calling it a day. It was a terrible loss to the City and to Wales because the lad could really play.

Mr Jones did a strange bit of business when he traded Johnny Watkins for my Wales team-mate Dai Ward and a few thousand pounds. Johnny told me that he wanted to get back to Bristol but I really believed Cardiff would try to keep him as he had proved a very good player. With Derek Hogg at the club, perhaps Mr Jones thought he could manage without Johnny.

I was called upon to play in goals when Newcastle United came to Ninian Park in the February. Graham Moore converted my cross to open the scoring and then I was brought down in the area for a stonewall penalty. Everyone stopped waiting for the referee to blow his whistle except Brian Walsh who knocked the loose ball into the net to put us two up. My old Wales team-mate Ivor Allchurch played very well for them and he scored just before half time to bring them back in the game. Graham scored another straight after the break and then came a collision between Maurice Swan and their winger, Gordon Hughes. Maurice should have gone off immediately but he stayed on and United took advantage with Len White making it 3-2. After that goal Maurice was forcibly removed by Wilf Grant and I took over in goal.

I collected a couple of crosses quite well and really enjoyed being between the sticks. While I was there, Barry Hole was injured and needed attention off the field and we were down to nine men but fortunately he returned after treatment. We held on to win and I never conceded a goal.

On 11 March, over 45,000 fans crammed into the ground for a Saturday evening match against league leaders Tottenham Hotspur. It was an incredible day in Cardiff because that afternoon, the Wales rugby team had met Ireland at Cardiff Arms Park in front of another 40,000 or so.

The football match more than lived up to the occasion. They were a good side with the record to prove it but we had 11 players who fought and fought. We were a goal down before we had even settled ourselves when little Terry Dyson scored. Then Derek Hogg went on a dribble through the centre and beat a couple of Spurs defenders before shooting in to the top corner but Les Allen quickly put them back in front. We came out in the second half to the roar of the crowd and it really made the difference as within about ten minutes Daisy had equalised and then I met a low cross at the near post to stab in the winner. You would have thought we had won the cup the noise was so deafening. Danny Malloy and Ron Nicholls in goal were superb as we held out until the end despite some heavy challenges from Dave Mackay and Bobby Smith. After the game it was good to renew some old friendships in the players lounge over a cup of tea.

That match seemed to take all our energy as we failed to win any of our last nine games to finish our first season back at the top in 15th place. I was top scorer with 21 league goals followed by Peter Donnelly with seven.

Before winding down, we went on a short tour to Ireland where we played two matches, drawing 2-2 with Shamrock Rovers and beating Waterford 5-1.

On 12 July, Glen gave birth to our first daughter at Glossop Terrace, an annexe of the Cardiff Royal Infirmary. Seeing Glen and baby Karen together was even better than scoring a hat-trick at Ninian Park. The summer lay-off went very quickly now that I was a family man.

14

RELEGATION BLUES AND FACES FROM THE PAST

In my opinion we were relegated before the season had even begun because of the club's penny-pinching attitude. During the summer, Jimmy Hill and the Players Union had successfully fought to have the maximum wage removed. When we returned to Ninian Park to start pre-season work we were all told that everyone would be on the same money. What the club could have said was that we would all be on £30 per week, a rise of £5. Bearing in mind that we had never received a bonus for winning promotion, there were a lot of disgruntled players.

The money offered was not acceptable to Danny Malloy who felt that as captain he should have a little extra. The club refused to pay him the small amount he wanted and so he left to join Doncaster Rovers as player-manager. It was a sad loss as Danny had played a very important part in City's promotion and first season in Division One and it was to prove a decisive blow to our hopes of staying in the top division.

I was left in the reserves for the opening games as Johnny King had been purchased from Stoke City and he was preferred up front in my position. I was brought in for the 3-2 defeat at White Hart Lane but scored the following week as we thumped Chelsea 5-2 at Ninian Park. But the clouds began gathering when we had only managed three victories, two of those against bottom-club Chelsea, in our first 11 matches.

We picked up a little after that although I missed the 1-1 draw with Arsenal through injury. Then I scored the only goal of the game at Fulham followed by a couple in the 2-1 win over Sheffield Wednesday and suddenly we were up to seventh in the table. From then on it really was all downhill. A few weeks later, the club made the astonishing decision to sell Graham Moore to relegation threatened Chelsea for £35,000 and even though Mel Charles was brought in from Arsenal for £28,000, he couldn't stem the tide. We did however receive a small increase in pay on his arrival. Mel had obviously refused to accept the standard wage so the club gave us all a rise.

A Friday night fixture at home to Fulham put the final nail in the coffin. Bill Jones and Wilf Grant took us to the Waters Edge, a hotel in Barry, to key us up for the vital game. All it did was make us even more tense and nervous and as a result, Fulham won 3-0. I'm pretty confident that if we had won that game, we would have stayed up as the Londoners finished the season only one point better off than us.

Easter brought us a little hope with matches against West Ham and Birmingham City at Ninian Park. Good Friday had seen us well-beaten 4-1 at Upton Park but when Birmingham came on the Saturday I notched up my second Division One hat-trick for the Bluebirds and we won 3-2. I scored another goal as we beat the Hammers 3-0 in the return match on the Monday to give ourselves just the tiniest hope that we could avoid relegation, but we had a rude awakening at Everton next time out and were swamped 8-3 at Goodison. There was no escape after that, we were going down.

Two seasons before we had sampled what it was like to be promoted and now we found what the other side of the coin was like and I can tell you I know which one I preferred. It wasn't a very nice feeling to know that you had failed and in the process, let down an awful lot of supporters.

The club reduced our wages after relegation and in some cases it was by quite a bit. Strike action was called for at one stage and most of the first team squad didn't sign contracts until the start of the season.

There was a lot of activity on the transfer front before the start of life in Division Two. Johnny King and Dai Ward left for pastures new and in came hard-shooting winger Peter Hooper and Wales international Ivor Allchurch who was surprisingly allowed to leave Newcastle. Once again I found myself out in the cold for the early games as the three central spots in attack were filled by Alan Durban, Mel Charles and Ivor.

I thought about going in to see Mr Jones to find out my position but decided against it as he had a lot to worry about. I came back into the side on 1 September but nine days later Mr Jones and trainer Wilf Grant were both dismissed. It was the first time in the club's history that the manager had been sacked. What appeared to have happened was that a director came into the dressing room after the midweek match against Swansea at the Vetch Field which we lost 2-1 and found Wilf Grant giving us all a rollicking while Mr Jones stood to one side. The director obviously thought that it should be Mr Jones doing the shouting and must have reported what happened at the next board meeting. Whatever, the result was still the same, the manager was sacked. I was surprised that Wilf had to go as well because he was doing a good job and we all respected his efforts.

Ron Stitfall and Ernie Curtis took control of team affairs on a temporary basis and things began to look a little rosier for a time. Ernie had played for the club in the 1927 cup final and was another who was well respected by everyone. We beat Preston 6-2, Scunthorpe 4-0 and Southampton 5-3 and I got among the goals. Rotherham were the visitors in early November and we romped to a 4-1 victory to put us all in good heart for the trip to the Valley and Charlton Athletic the following Saturday.

Training that week went very well as it seemed that the improvement in results had lifted a heavy load off us but we had all heard the rumours that a new manager would shortly be appointed and a few likely names had been bandied about. On the Friday I was doing some lap work around the pitch with Mel Charles when one of the Cardiff directors came out of the tunnel. He saw us near by and called us both over.

'Have you heard about the new appointment?' he said. I told him that I hoped it wasn't going to be the person I had heard could be given the job. Then the bottom fell out of my world when Mel and I were told that the new manager was going to be George Swindin, the very man who got rid of both us when he was in charge at the Arsenal, and who wanted a fight with me in the dressing room after a match between the clubs.

I sat with Mel on the train as we went from Cardiff to Paddington the following day and there in London to meet us on the coach taking us to the Valley was Mr Swindin.

He introduced himself to the players but Mel and I quickly sat together as no way were we going to talk to him.

Funnily enough, we put aside all our worries during the game, slammed Charlton 4-2 and I scored another hat-trick. In the dressing room after the game Mr Swindin said 'Thanks lads, you did that for me.' I looked him squarely in the eye and said that I had scored the three goals for Derek Tapscott and for Cardiff City.

One good move Mr Swindin made was to bring Stan Montgomery to the club as the new trainer although Ernie Curtis stayed on the coaching staff. Stan thought Swindin was a good manager who struggled a little because Bill Jones and Wilf Grant before him were such popular figures. Just as he was finding his feet the big freeze put a stop to football and we didn't play for two long months. It was difficult trying to keep fit during that time as we were unable to go out on long runs and had to be content with training in and around Ninian Park.

The club did have a well appointed treatment room. It was situated along the corridor from the dressing rooms in an area now used as the manager's office. By today's standards it sounds very old-fashioned but it contained infra-red, radiant heat and short-wave machines, a static bicycle for leg work, and a rowing machine for strengthening back muscles. The only problem was that you had to wait your turn.

When football resumed I kept my place in the side and only missed a few games through injury, so Mr Swindin was playing fair by me. But I was starting to find that knocks were taking longer to clear up. It was a sort of catch 22 situation. I was a yard slower than I used to be because of injuries so now I was getting to the ball the same time as the defender. This meant that I was suffering more injuries and so it went on in a vicious circle.

At the end of the season Mr Swindin transfer-listed 13 players, six of us with international experience. He said that he was forced to sell in order to buy. In actual fact, there were some who were more than ready to leave because they had been told their wages would be cut by up to £10 a week for the next season. 'The club cannot afford Division One wages while playing in Division Two,' he told us. That summer was definitely not a happy one though I relieved a little of the stress by getting a summer job. With Alan Harrington and a couple of the other lads I went and worked for a month at Cathays Cemetery cutting the grass and generally tidying the area up. It kept us active and meant that we were in reasonably good shape when we returned for pre-season training.

Peter Hooper, Alan Durban and Maurice Swan were just some of the players who left the club before the start of the

1963-64 season. John Charles arrived in Cardiff for talks and when centre half Frank Rankmore was allowed to join Peterborough, it was inevitable that Charlo would sign for the Bluebirds. That proved to be a real boost for the club because although Big John had reached his peak in Italy, he was still a very formidable player. I read much later that George Swindin opposed the signing of Charlo because he thought it would increase the average age of the team too much.

Alec Milne broke his leg in a pre-season friendly and then in the public trial where Firsts played against the Reserves, Alan Harrington and Trevor Peck both suffered broken legs and we were already in trouble before we had even started.

Once again my season would begin in the Combination with the reserves as Mr Swindin used Dick Scott, a new signing from Norwich City, at number nine for the first couple of games. I was in for the visit to Scunthorpe and popped up with the winner in a 2-1 success. A calf strain kept me out of the next match against Manchester City but I returned for a run of six successive games after that.

I played against Portsmouth in a 2-1 defeat and suffered a bang on my foot and it caused me a lot of trouble during the next run of matches. After scoring twice in a 2-2 Football League Cup draw with Wrexham at Ninian Park, my foot gave me even more trouble and I was sent to hospital for an x-ray. It revealed the surprising news that I had broken bones in my foot in the Portsmouth game and I had played another five matches with that handicap. My foot was put in plaster and I was laid up for six weeks. Mind you I had plenty of company as Alec Milne, Alan Harrington and Trevor Peck were all still in plaster as well.

Despite any misgivings I may have had, I must say that Mr Swindin was very meticulous in his preparation for games. He would study the opposition and advise each player on how best to play that particular match. You could tell he had been schooled in the right place because he rarely used bad language. In fact he had a rather amusing phrase that he used quite often. Where other men would swear, Mr Swindin would say 'Christopher Columbus' and look up to the heavens. That was sufficient release for him to get something out of his system and was probably learnt during his many years at the Arsenal.

I came back briefly in a 2-1 win over Huddersfield, was left out again, and then had a run of seven or eight games but the season was over for me by the end of February and it was probably the least productive of any during my career as a footballer. The only league goal I scored was the one at Scunthorpe although I did get the two against Wrexham and one in an early round of the Welsh Cup against Chester.

On 15 February 1964 I travelled in the team bus going to Northampton Town for a league match. We had just reached Chepstow when a police car flagged us to a stop. The bus door opened and a policeman's head popped in and said 'We've come for Mr Tapscott. His wife has gone into labour.' That was a big shock for me because Glen wasn't due for another couple of weeks. I jumped off the bus, said cheerio and best of luck to the lads, and sped off in the police car back to Cardiff where Glen gave birth that day to another daughter we called Jayne.

When Glen first began having the pains she had asked a neighbour to look after Karen, our three-year-old, and then another neighbour was press-ganged into taking her into the nursing home in North Road. Everything turned out alright and both mother and baby recovered really well.

At the end of the season we reached the final of the Welsh Cup but lost 2-0 at Bangor City before winning the second leg 3-1.

The day before the third and deciding match, which was played at the Racecourse, we were given the shock news that Mr Swindin had been relieved of his duties. Apparently, after a stormy board meeting he was asked to resign but refused. The board then decided to sack him immediately.

We won the play-off 2-0 but I was not included in any of the three final matches and never felt part of that particular success even though I had played in previous rounds.

The new addition to the family kept my mind off a poor injury-hit season under Mr Swindin but now I was going to have to prove my worth to a new man. We didn't have long to wait to find out who that was going to be.

The Welsh Cup victory was significant however as it meant that Cardiff City would be playing in the European Cup Winners Cup the following season.

All the retained players were called to Ninian Park at the end of June to meet the new manager. Into the room came Jimmy Scoular, the same Jimmy Scoular who had kicked me all over St James' Park in my third game for Arsenal at Newcastle way back in 1954. I didn't know whether to laugh or cry. First of all I had to contend with George Swindin who had got rid of me from Arsenal, and now my new manager was going to be Mr Scoular who had left me black and blue after that game on Tyneside.

It was time to put all my energy into another little summer job. For some reason we couldn't do the cemetery grass cutting so along with Alan Harrington once again, I took a job as a builder's labourer working on a new shopping precinct in Wood Street, Cardiff. It took me back to the time I worked for Barry Council just about ten years earlier. We weren't very good at it though and it took us a whole day to fill a lorry with builders waste. I think they were glad to see the back of us after four weeks.

15

EUROPE, NEWPORT AND THE FOREST OF DEAN

It soon became clear that Mr Scoular was totally different to George Swindin. He had joined Cardiff from Bradford where he was player-manager and in fact played in the league the season before coming to the City and hanging up his boots.

The one trouble we did have with him was that he still thought of himself as a player and would join in all the five-a-sides. He thought nothing of crashing into you with hard tackles, just as he used to do when playing in his Portsmouth and Newcastle days. If you didn't follow suit the same way he would shout and swear and Mr Scoular's language was very often quite colourful and could honestly be described as 'industrial'. If we were playing 11-a-side, he would continue with the match until the side he was playing on ended up as winners. There used to be some tired legs after training with Mr Scoular. To be fair, he was quite straight and honest with all of us and we knew exactly where we stood.

He had a big row with Ernie Curtis over his robust methods and it ended with Ernie finishing at the club. Ron Stitfall wasn't too keen on Mr Scoular either. He thought that he terrorised the young players too much and as Ron ran the Youth team at that time he didn't want his young charges demoralised. Even though you have given 25 years service to the club it means nothing if you can't get on with the manager so Ron left to take the well-worn route to Newport.

A lot of the senior professionals had difficulties with the manager. The player who suffered the most was Ivor Allchurch who had been at Newcastle with Scoular. After being left out of the starting line-up for half the 1964-65 season he became disillusioned at his treatment and left to re-join Swansea Town.

Just after the start of the season the club began a lottery which was called B.I.F. The letters stood for Bluebirds Improvement Fund and it was based on numbered tickets with the winning numbers published every day in the South Wales Echo and South Wales Argus. The club wanted someone to help promote the sale of the tickets and I took over the running of the fund from a little office inside Ninian Park. Soon after another lottery started called B.A.F. This was the Bluebirds Auxiliary Fund and Colin Baker came in to run that side.

We would travel all over South Wales trying to get agents to take on the sale of the tickets and eventually we were quite successful. The tickets cost 1s (5p) each, and the top prize during the week was £20 but on Saturday that was increased to £50. Colin and I would do all our paperwork in the afternoons after training.

Despite Mr Scoular's hard work and good intentions, the early results didn't go our way and we went 12 games before winning our first match against Derby County at Ninian Park. Peter King scored one and I grabbed what turned out to be the winner.

Fortunately, we had the Cup Winners Cup to look forward to and in September we travelled to Denmark where we met Esbjerg in the first round. It was not the first time the club had played in that little fishing port because on a club tour in 1959 we had beaten them 4-0 and I scored a hat-trick, but I was the only survivor of that trip still with the City.

It was very misty when we flew from Cardiff (Rhoose)

Airport for the first leg. Confidence was high although at that time we were second from bottom in Division Two with only three points. The Danish club provided us with good accommodation and there were no complaints from any of us about the food. The conditions at the ground were a bit primitive but we knew we had a job to do.

I was a bit disappointed to be left out of the starting line-up but Mr Scoular explained that he was going for a defensive display in the away leg but it would be changed when the teams met at Ninian Park. His tactics worked perfectly and we drew 0-0 out there although we really should have beaten them. The second leg didn't take place until the middle of October. Charlo was injured and his place taken by young Don Murray who was a chip off the Scoular block. I was pleased because I regained my place as leader of the attack and knew I would be kept busy because of course we had to score to go through to the next round. After a bit of a struggle we won 1-0 with a header by Peter King from a Greg Farrell cross. That game meant I was pretty sure I had become the first Welshman to play in two different European competitions, the Inter-Cities Fairs cup with London and now the Cup Winners cup. The only disappointment came in the size of the crowd for the first European match at Ninian Park. At 8,000, Cardiff fans were not yet convinced by European football.

By now our league position was rock bottom although we had just won that first match against Derby. I was being given a decent run up front and managed to score the only goal of the game against Portsmouth and then hit a double in a 4-0 win over Bury with Keith Ellis and Bernard Lewis scoring the others. After the horror start we were now playing well, moving up the table, and I was hitting the back of the net fairly regularly.

Next up was the second round of the Cup Winners Cup and we had been given the hardest draw of all when we were paired with Sporting Lisbon, the holders of the trophy. The first leg was played at the Estadio Jose Alvalade, the old stadium not the one used during Euro 2004. We stayed in a hotel that was owned by Fulham chairman Ernie Clay in the hills above Lisbon.

They were a bruising side, typically continental in their approach, with shirt tugging, obstruction and tripping the order of the day. Charlo played at sweeper once again as Mr Scoular thought his experience of continental football would help at the back. He suffered for it though as he was butted early on and needed four stitches in a head wound. The referee was Mr Kreitlein of West Germany and he gave us no protection whatsoever. He was a bit different the following year during the World Cup at Wembley when he sent off Argentina skipper Rattin in the match against England.

We shocked the home crowd by opening the scoring on the half hour when I worked my way down the field with Peter King. The ball went inside to Greg Farrell who beat the keeper with a good low shot. In the second half I doubled the lead with a goal that I could never repeat even if I tried it a hundred times. Greg swung a ball out to me on the right wing. I moved to go down the line but their centre half came across to block me. Looking up I saw Bernard Lewis running into a good position on the edge of the area so I decided to swing over a cross to him. I overhit the ball and it went towards their near post and the keeper seemed to lose sight of it. When he eventually saw it coming it was too late and he pushed it into the net off the post. Although they pulled one back late on, we managed to keep them out to take a 2-1 lead back to Ninian Park. Don Murray was really coming of age at centre half under the expert teaching of Charlo and he played very well against an experienced attack.

Before the second leg which was one week later, Mr Scoular had us all together to talk through our tactics for the game. He was going to play the same side but expected us to be put under a lot of pressure so we all had to be prepared to work hard and do plenty of running. That game plan suited me because that was the way I liked to play. Charlo and young Don were magnificent once again and they hardly had a look-in around our penalty area. I was given a bit of a buffeting by their players and needed a couple of stitches in a cut over my right eye after their keeper decided to punch me along with the ball after one attack. If there is ever a photograph of that game printed anywhere then it always seems to be the one showing me sat in the dressing room with a sticky plaster over the cut. If I had a £1 for every time that photo was reproduced I would be a very rich man. We held out fairly comfortably for a 0-0 draw and the holders were out of the competition. There was nothing to complain about with the size of the crowd either as 25,000, the best attendance of the season to date, were at Ninian Park to cheer us on to victory.

Next up were Real Zaragoza, holders of the Inter-Cities Fairs Cup, the competition in which I had represented London way back in my Arsenal days, but that was not until after Christmas.

Five days before the first leg in Zaragoza we thrashed Middlesbrough 6-1 for one of our biggest ever wins and I cracked in another double. Little did I know at the time that they would be the last first team goals I would score for Cardiff City. Peter King was developing into a good midfield schemer and he bagged a hat-trick that day with the skipper, Gareth Williams, scoring the other. Peter had been included in place of Ivor Allchurch and more than justified his selection. It put us in good heart for the trip to Spain but we were told that Real were second in La Liga and unbeaten at home that season.

Once again we were put up in a good standard hotel and were able to train at their stadium before the match. Charlo knew La Romareda well as he told me he had played there

169

before for Roma in the Fairs Cup. Mr Scoular brought in Bob Wilson, a new signing from Villa – not the more famous Arsenal keeper of the same name. He was in goal in place of Dilwyn John and that was the only change from the side that played against Sporting. I got on very well with Bob and we roomed together in Zaragoza.

The game didn't go to plan and we found ourselves two down inside quarter of an hour. Their first came after 60 seconds following a foul by Gareth Williams when the free kick was lashed beyond Bob and into the net. Ten minutes later we seemed down and out when they doubled their lead.

One thing Mr Scoular had already instilled in us was never to give in. Greg Farrell started tormenting their defenders and from his cross Gareth pulled one back. Just before half time we levelled when Peter King headed a Farrell cross high into the net. Once again they tried all means to regain the lead but we rode the storm to come away with a 2-2 draw.

The league fixtures had not been very kind to us and when we returned from Spain on the Thursday, there was very little time to prepare for the trip to Newcastle where we had to meet United on the Saturday. Needless to say it was a tired team that were beaten 2-0 that day, much to the disappointment of Mr Scoular who dearly wanted to put one over his old club.

Ninian Park was packed for the visit of Zaragoza and the crowd of 38,500 was the biggest of the season. The match began very well for us and the Spanish side played very defensively and we seemed to get on top in the first half. I decided to get after their keeper and gave him a bit of a bang every time he caught the ball. This only brought the worst out of their defenders and I received a lot of punishment with kicks off the ball which the referee did not see, or if he did, turned a blind eye. After I made one move on the keeper three or four of their players came after me and a linesman had to rush on to drag them off me. That could have been really nasty. Just when we thought that the game was there for the winning, their right wing Canario cut through and planted the ball in the net to give them a 3-2 aggregate victory. He was a former Real Madrid player but still shouldn't have been given the time and space to get his shot in. It was a disappointing end but the club had really done well in a first attempt at European football.

There were very few footballers playing the game with a similar style to mine but Cardiff City unearthed one likely candidate when a little Scottish teenager called Georgie Johnston came to the club from Glasgow. He played on the wing but could also operate inside, just like me, and he wasn't afraid of getting stuck in and doing his share of tackling and chasing. After he had been with the club for a few months and found his feet, he came to the B.I.F. office one afternoon for a chat. He had watched the first team in action and knew for himself that our styles were similar.

'What do I have to do to achieve all the things that you have done in football?' he asked. Straightaway my mind went back to when I was first starting out and the advice I was given by Charlie Dyke and Stan Richards at Barry and then Tommy Lawton and Joe Mercer at the Arsenal. I told him that the only way to get on was to work hard, listen to advice, and live sensibly, and that meant looking after your body. After that I kept an eye on him especially during Combination matches and I could see that the lad had a lot of talent and could go a long way if he looked after himself. Unfortunately, even in those days, drink could get a hold of you and it was easy to slip into bad habits. It was very disappointing to find in later years that George hadn't taken the advice to heart. He earned himself a dream move to Arsenal from Cardiff but soon fell by the wayside because he wasn't prepared to make sufficient sacrifices.

I cannot understand the present-day drinking culture that

surrounds the game. You cannot combine football, or any other sport, with drinking even in moderation. How is it that clubs leave their players open to temptation by taking them away for a mid-season break to foreign hotels where boredom inevitably leads to a visit to the bar?

My last first team game in a Bluebird shirt was a 2-0 home defeat by Northampton Town on 6 February, 1965. Northampton went on that year to win promotion to the First Division under my old Arsenal colleague Dave Bowen but it was only a brief rise to the top as in a few short years they were back down in Division Four.

I had played in only 16 games by then but had managed to score eight league goals. Injury kept me out of the starting line-up the following week and I was unable to win my place back.

On the Thursday of the last week of the season I was busy in the B.I.F. office when Graham Keenor, the club secretary, came in to find out a few figures for that afternoon's board meeting. I had them all ready and he thanked me for the work I was doing to promote the lottery. Later on that afternoon, at the end of the board meeting, he brought the paperwork back to me.

The following day I had a letter from Cardiff City Football Club telling me that my services as a player were no longer required. It went on to say that I could still carry on promoting the club lottery providing I retired as a player.

I found it incredible that the club secretary and directors knew I was at the ground late the day before, yet none of them had the guts to come and tell me that I was no longer wanted at the club. There was no way that I would have continued running the lottery but that presented a problem as my name as promoter was on all the tickets. I made a quick phone call to my solicitor and he said he would instruct the club that they could not sell lottery tickets with my name on them. To be perfectly honest, at the time I hoped it would cause them a few problems because I was totally disgusted with my treatment after I had given them six years wholehearted service. As it happened, they had to have new tickets printed and it did cost them a little bit of money.

During the summer I spent time with Glen and the girls wondering what I was going to do. Neither of us wanted to move away from Cardiff but I needed to be working.

The football grapevine works very fast and I received a telephone call from Les Courtier, manager of Addington FC in South Africa during which he asked me if I would be interested in continuing my career over there.

This was followed in a few days by a letter from the club setting out terms together with a contract ready for me to sign. I must admit I was tempted by a very good offer but the down payment of £1,000 that would be due to me would only be put into my account once I was in South Africa. It was also confirmed that while I had to go almost immediately by air, all expenses paid, Glen and our two little girls would have to travel out later. We decided that it was too much of a risk, especially with the country in a state of unrest.

We also had a call from Sligo Rovers in Ireland and they wanted me to become player-manager of their club but that never appealed to either of us and I never took that offer very far.

Then out of the blue I received a telephone call from Billy Lucas, manager of nearby Newport County, asking me to pop down to the club for a chat. I had known Billy for some time as our paths crossed occasionally at charity football matches.

A day or so later I met him at Somerton Park and he sold me on the idea of starting the next season, 1965-66, with the County. It seemed ideal as it was a route that Cardiff City players had taken for many years and it would not mean having to uproot the family. My best pal from Arsenal and Cardiff days, Brian Walsh, had gone to County from Cardiff but only stayed a season before retiring. I never thought of giving him a ring and asking him about the club, after all that was three or four years previously. But maybe I should have done because going to Newport turned out to be the biggest mistake in my life.

My first game in County's amber colours was against Rochdale at Somerton Park at the end of August. I knew Ken Morgans, from his time at Manchester United so at least there was one familiar face. They were a typical lower division side with a couple of decent players but it was back-to-the-walls stuff for most of the season as you would expect from a club that had finished in the lower half of Division Four the previous year.

That first match ended with me struggling with a leg injury and I was unfit to be considered once again until November. By then Billy Lucas had bought Alfie Hale from Doncaster and he took over up front until my return. I missed the 3-0 win over Darlington and the next match was in the FA Cup.

The club was drawn against Southern League side Bath City at their place and the whole squad were on the coach as we left Somerton Park early for the short trip to the west country. When we arrived at their ground the directors and manager went off to find the nearest watering hole and we went to the away dressing room to wait for the team announcement. With less than an hour to go before kick-off, no team announcement had been made and I asked Ray Wilcox the trainer if he knew what the side was. He looked a little embarrassed as he said he didn't know for sure but thought that it would be an unchanged team from the win over Darlington. I was unhappy to say the least and left the dressing room to go outside and wait for Billy Lucas to get back to the ground. A short time later he turned up and his first words were 'Why aren't you changed?' I told him it was because we weren't sure of the team. When I followed him into the dressing room he said to everyone there, 'The same team as last week lads,' so that meant I wasn't playing and didn't need to get changed. Had I known that I wouldn't have travelled.

After they lost that cup-tie 2-0 to Bath, I was selected for a good run in the side but it was not until the middle of November that I was on a winning team for the County when we beat Aldershot 3-1 at Somerton Park. By now a certain amount of friction had developed between me and the County management.

I wasn't happy at Newport. When I joined I knew full well that the standards would not be those I had been accustomed to at Arsenal or even Cardiff City. If you drop down to the bottom division then it is only natural that conditions are not on a par with the top level. Yet I couldn't come to terms with the lack of discipline at the club particularly with regards to training. I was used to being on time for training, and at Arsenal and Cardiff, particularly in Jimmy Scoular's day, there was no way you would want to be late for training because if you were, you were certainly made to suffer. At Newport however players seemed to decide for themselves when to turn up.

It wasn't so much the actual work done during training it was the slaphappy way the players seemed to treat what is a vitally important part of a professional's life.

I played in half-a-dozen games either side of Christmas but was then injured once again and had to take a back seat until returning about the middle of February.

On 7 March, 1966 I scored my one and only league goal for County when we beat Bradford 3-1 at Somerton Park with Ken Morgans scoring the others. That was a bit of a weight lifted from me but at Doncaster I was injured again, causing me to have another lay-off and start thinking about calling it a day. I was 34 and had been knocked about a bit so I thought the time may be right to hang up the boots.

My last game for County was over the Easter period when I received yet another knock during the 3-0 defeat at Vale Park and left the field to be substituted by Polly Rowland.

I decided there and then to call a halt to playing league football.

For the remaining month of the season I concentrated on getting myself fit because I knew I would be no use to Glen and the girls if I spent the entire summer limping about the house being miserable.

Then out of the blue in July, I received a lovely letter from solicitors acting on behalf of Sliema Wanderers, a top side in Malta. They offered me a good salary and a furnished flat provided for the whole family to become the club's player-manager. Income tax would also be paid by the club and they also promised to provide good schooling for the girls. It was a very tempting offer and Glen and I thought long and hard about it. In those days Malta wasn't in the holiday brochures so we didn't know too much about the island. It became easier to refuse when I was told of another offer.

I was still going to charity matches with the Good Sports XI and while I was at one, Neil Jordan and Tommy Rees, two old pals who owned sports shops, suggested I contact Gola Sports. Apparently, they were looking for suitable former professionals with good contacts to show off their sports goods. I contacted them straightaway and was taken on. After a short spell of initial training, I was travelling all over West Wales, the West Country and up as far as Hereford showing off the company's range of sports goods.

I used to pick up new stock such as boots, tracksuits, training gear and all that sort of stuff and take them around the sports shops.

Just before the start of the 1966-67 season, I had a call from an old friend called Johnny Preece. He was manager of Cinderford Town who were based in the Forest of Dean. I had first met Johnny when I was a drill instructor in

Aldershot during my army days. Johnny had arrived at the base for the very first time with someone he had met up with from Barry and it was this lad who had told Johnny who I was. Just as I was drilling a new set of conscripts on the parade ground, I heard someone shout out 'Tappy!'

I immediately collared this new recruit and made him do a couple of hours on the parade ground as punishment for shouting out my name. After that we became great friends but his phone call from Cinderford came out of the blue.

I met him in Lydney where I had a Gola customer. I told him I had just starting working for them and he said that would fit in very well with what he had in mind. It turned out that I was offered as much money at Cinderford as in my last season at Cardiff City. So with my proper job as well, I was in clover.

I was now very busy representing a sports firm during the week and playing for Cinderford at weekends. Johnny even saw to it that I was paid expenses for all the travelling from Cardiff. They had a lovely little ground deep in the Forest of Dean.

I scored both goals against Redditch in a 2-1 win and then hit all four as we defeated Shrewsbury Town Reserves 4-0. It was a good feeling to give something back to a club and supporters that had made me feel so very welcome. I was to stay for two seasons with Cinderford but then found that as my main employment was taking up more of my time, travelling up to the Midlands particularly for away matches was beginning to be impossible.

Barry John had now joined the Gola team and rugby boots were added to the list. Barry had many contacts and he would let me know what size of boots he wanted and I would collect them from the warehouse. Emlyn Hughes and a few of the Liverpool lads began wearing Gola boots and they became very fashionable so life for me was quite busy and rewarding.

I had intended to finish playing once and for all when my old pal Mel Charles came to see me. He was playing with Haverfordwest in the Welsh League and he persuaded me to carry on for a little longer. I enjoyed it at first but when Ivor Allchurch also joined the club and slowly began bringing in Swansea lads, I felt it was time to move on. That was no disrespect to Ivor who had every right to bring in local lads.

I went to Carmarthen Town but only stayed a short time as the enjoyment of playing had completely gone. In any case, they always expected me to take a couple of players with me to most games. So at 39 years of age, I decided once and for all to hang up my boots.

16

LIFE WITHOUT FOOTBALL

I never stopped playing completely because there was still the Goods Sports XI. We played against sides such as Alf Sherwood's XI, all in aid of good causes. We usually played once a month and the likes of Trevor Ford, Stan Stennett and Johnny Preece would be regulars in our team. Every year we would hold a big dinner dance at the Marina in Penarth. All the stars would turn up and we made loads of money for good causes. Without regular football however, I was also able to play much more golf.

I stayed with Gola Sports for about five years until I was offered a better position with an Italian company called Diadora. I went to their UK head office in Dorking and they must have been satisfied with my record as I got the job. Diadora had become the main suppliers in this country of track suits, playing kit, footballs, boots and bags.

In time I attended exhibitions in London and Bournemouth, and even put on my own shows in hotels in and around Cardiff. One of my customers in Bristol was Norman Hunter, the former Leeds and England player. We used to talk business for five minutes and then football for a couple of hours.

They were good times and I enjoyed working for Diadora as it seemed that I was still very much involved in football. I stayed with them until I retired at the age of 65 in 1997.

Just before I retired, London Weekend Television contacted me to film me at home for a sports programme.

They spent the best part of the day with us, we provided food for them and they used our electricity for the filming. When they finished I asked if I could have a copy of the programme and was told that it would cost me £300 so I didn't bother. I should have given them a cheque for that amount and then charged them £300 for the catering and power.

By this time the family had another sport to get interested in as both my daughters were excellent basketball and netball players. So much so that Karen and Jayne both represented Wales at under-15 level and on up through the other age groups as well. It was a very proud moment for us when the girls first represented their country and throughout their involvement with the national team we were thrilled that they had done so well. Jayne had a degree from Loughborough University and now lives in Bahrain with husband Nigel and our grandson Haydn. Karen and husband Paul are not so far away in Cheltenham where her two boys Jamie and Gareth are both football mad. Jamie is at present going to Leicester City on a regular basis for football training but whether he will end up good enough to follow his granddad, only time will tell.

Dad passed away in March 1975 after a long illness and then in July 1996 we lost mam. Although she had a hard life bringing up 16 children she lived to the ripe old age of 91 and when she died she had 120 children, grandchildren and great grandchildren.

I am very pleased that the Arsenal Football Club have never forgotten me. Whenever there is something coming up where they would like former players to attend they are always in touch. The most recent time was on the fiftieth anniversary of my debut against Liverpool which was in April 2004. I had a phone call from the editor of the Arsenal programme who wanted an interview as they were going to put an article about me in the programme for the match against Liverpool. I was doubly pleased as Cardiff City also had a couple of pages in their programme at about the same time.

In December 1986, I was invited to Highbury for a match against Southampton which also commemorated 100 years of the Arsenal club. Loads of former players were there and it was good to see them and talk over old times. We were all paraded out on the pitch before the match and given a tremendous reception by the crowd.

Two weeks later, 4 January, Glen and I were back in London to celebrate the 100th match between Spurs and Arsenal. We were looked after very well and this time both sets of former players lined up on either side of each other before being presented to the crowd. Afterwards I had long chats about old times with Joe Mercer, Dennis Evans, Ted Ditchburn and Danny Blanchflower. Joe had always kept in touch with me and seemed very interested in how I was getting on. We also met up with Bill Dodgin and it was good to find out that he was still a keen opera and ballet lover. Glen and I stayed with our old friends George Gibson and his wife as he still lived close to Highbury.

Every time Arsenal reached a cup final we were given two tickets. We went to Wembley in 1978 when we lost 1-0 to Ipswich Town and then back again the following year when we beat Manchester United 3-2 in a very exciting match. It brought back vivid memories of when I played at Wembley for Wales against England many years before. We only had the two tickets so I went to watch the United match with Jayne, who was 14 at the time, while Glen and Karen, now nearly 17, toured the West End shops.

I had always been interested in boxing, though Glen wasn't too keen, particularly after that trip to Maindy Stadium to see Dick Richardson and Dai Dower so many years ago. In October 1989 I was sent tickets by the National Sporting Club who put on a number of bouts as a tribute evening for Arsenal. The proceeds all went to the

Commonwealth Games Appeal Fund. I found that attending events such as these was one way of giving something back.

Less than a month later we were back in London for a dinner to celebrate Jack Kelsey's retirement after 40 years service to Arsenal. There were so many former players and current stars of television, music and films that it was a job knowing where to start to name them all.

My most recent invitation from the Arsenal came for the first cup final at the Millennium Stadium when Arsenal played Liverpool. By this time there were so many former players that we were asked to buy the tickets but I didn't mind that one bit. It was the first time I had been to the Millennium Stadium and it really is a fantastic arena to play football.

Not long after that I developed a few breathing problems and have since needed treatment in hospital on a few occasions. It has curtailed my visits to London and even trips to Ninian Park although I did go once last season. I went on to the pitch before a match with my pal Brian Clark and Ronnie Bird and we were introduced to the fans.

The illness has prevented me from playing golf which has been a big disappointment to my old friend Gethin Jones and his wife Zena. While Gethin partnered me around Whitchurch Golf course for many years, Glen and Zena used to meet up and enjoy each other's company. Gethin was with me when I hit holes-in-one on two successive weeks at the club. That was a very expensive couple of rounds.

Although I missed the game a lot when I first retired, I'm glad that I am not playing in this day and age. Much of the fun has gone out of the game and the cause of the problem is undoubtedly money. I watch a lot of football on television and I have been very disappointed with the lack of discipline shown by players during matches.

There was no way a player would shout and swear at the referee in my day and how the officials put up with the abuse thrown at them these days is beyond me.

It was a simpler game then although basically it is still played under the same rules. You may have seen Nat Lofthouse, Trevor Ford, or even Derek Tapscott charge the goalkeeper into the net, but did you ever see any of them go up and elbow an opponent in the head? Did you ever see a player rolling over and over after being fouled? There were far harder tacklers 30 or 40 years ago but if you were hurt, you didn't want to show it.

Referees have a duty to put a stop to all the play-acting and feigning of injury. It is a disgrace and could end up ruining the game because in time, tackling will not be allowed. Clubs should be made accountable for their players behaviour and if this means docking points then so be it.

When I was playing I was paid for doing something I enjoyed. I would have played for nothing. For someone coming from a family of 16 children I have been very lucky to have had the opportunity of playing at the highest level with, and against, the greatest players in the country. I have made loads of friends throughout football both at Arsenal and Cardiff and I am still asked for my autograph even now. Letters regularly come in the post with photos and requests for signatures and I am delighted that I am still remembered. I am very glad that while at Arsenal and Cardiff I took the time to stop and chat with fans and sign autographs. How many of today's pampered players can say that?

I have had a good life since taking that train ride to London with Bill Jones over 50 years ago.

DEREK TAPSCOTT PLAYING RECORD

Club	Appearances				Goals			
	League	FA Cup	Lge Cup	Others	League	FA Cup	Lge Cup	Others
Arsenal	119	13	-	-	62	6	-	-
Cardiff City	193	9	5	27	79	2	3	17
Newport Co.	15	-	-	-	1	-	-	-
327	**22**	**5**	**27**	**142**	**8**	**3**	**17**